MW00809441

Jefferson Davis
President of the Confederate States of America

STATE SOVEREIGNTY AND THE RIGHT OF SECESSION

An Historical and Constitutional
Defense of the Southern Position

by
Greg Loren Durand

Institute for Southern Historical Review
Toccoa, Georgia

State Sovereignty and the Right of Secession
An Historical and Constitutional Defense
of the Southern Position
by Greg Loren Durand

The contents of this book have been extracted from
America's Caesar: The Decline and Fall of Republican
Government in the United States of America
(Institute for Southern Historical Review, 2014)
to which is appended additional material.

Published by Institute for Southern Historical Review
Post Office Box 2027 Toccoa, Georgia 30577
www.southernhistoricalreview.org

Cover and Interior by Magnolia Graphic Design
www.magnoliagraphicdesign.com

ISBN-13: 978-0692488997
ISBN-10: 0692488995

The principle for which we contend is bound to reassert itself, though it may be at another time and in another form.

– C.S. President Jefferson Davis

There will come a time when the cry will ring across this land, "The cause of the South is the cause of us all!"

– C.S. Vice-President Alexander H. Stephens

CONTENTS

☆ ☆ ☆ ☆

CHAPTER ONE
The Union Viewed as an Experiment

In his excellent treatise on the nature of the Union entitled *Is Davis a Traitor?*, Southern political apologist Albert Taylor Bledsoe wrote, "The final judgment of History in relation to the war of 1861 will, in no small degree, depend on its verdict with respect to the right of secession. If, when this right was practically asserted by the South, it had been conceded by the North, there would not have been even a pretext for the tremendous conflict which followed."[1] Secession became the great political question of the Nineteenth Century to be decided, not by appealing to law and reason, which method Abraham Lincoln ridiculed as "exceedingly thin and airy,"[2] but, in the words of Supreme Court

---

1. Albert Taylor Bledsoe, *Is Davis a Traitor?* (Richmond, Virginia: The Hermitage Press, Inc., 1907), page 1.

2. John G. Nicolay and John Hay, *Abraham Lincoln: Complete Works* (New York: The Century Company, 1984), Volume I, page 673.

Justice Robert C. Grier, by "wager of Battle,"[3] or, to quote John Andrews, a radical Abolitionist who served as Governor of Massachusetts from 1861 to 1866, by "the logic of bayonets and rifles and pikes."[4]

From the formation of the original Confederacy under the Articles of Confederation of 1777, and continuing on after the ratification of the Constitution of 1789, it was a well-understood and universally accepted political doctrine that the Union was a compact, or a "league of friendship" between thirteen independent and sovereign States, from which the parties thereof could constitutionally and peacefully withdraw at will. According to Henry C. Lodge:

─────────────────

3. Justice Robert C. Grier, December 1862, *U.S. Reports*, Volume 67, page 668.

4. Speech delivered in Tremont Temple, Boston; New York *Herald*, December 1859. Andrews was an outspoken supporter of the fanatical assassin John Brown, who had attempted to incite servile insurrection throughout the Southern States in October of 1859. Brown's weapons of choice for the hoped-for wholesale murder of the families of Southern slaveholders were the rifles and pikes he attempted to confiscate from the Federal arsenal at Harper's Ferry, in what was then Virginia. Brown's plan was thwarted when he was captured by U.S. forces under the command of Colonel Robert E. Lee and then tried and hanged for treason by the Virginia authorities on 2 December 1859. An early song popular in the Union army included the lyrics, "John Brown's body lies a'mouldering in the grave, but his soul is marching on." This later evolved into Julia Ward Howe's famous "Battle Hymn of the Republic," in which the Southern people were likened to the "grapes of wrath" being trampled by the "coming of the Lord."

When the Constitution was adopted by the votes of States at Philadelphia, and accepted by the votes of States in popular conventions, it is safe to say there was no man in this country, from Washington and Hamilton on the one side to George Clinton and George Mason on the other, who regarded our system of Government, when first adopted, as anything but an experiment entered upon by the States, and from which each and every State had the right to peaceably withdraw, a right which was very likely to be exercised.[5]

The truth of Lodge's statement is established by George Washington himself, who, in his farewell address, asked, "Is there a doubt whether a common government can embrace so large a sphere? Let experience solve it. To listen to mere speculation in such a case were criminal. It is well worth a fair and full experiment." In his correspondence with various dignitaries, Washington constantly referred to the Union of States as "the new confederacy"[6] and a "confederated Government,"[7] and he spoke of the

---

5. Henry Cabot Lodge, *Daniel Webster* (Boston: Houghton, Mifflin, and Company, 1899), page 176.

6. Washington to General Pinckney, 28 June 1788; Bernard Janin Sage, *The Republic of Republics: A Retrospect of Our Century of Federal Liberty* (Philadelphia, Pennsylvania: William W. Harding, 1878), page 248.

7. Washington to Sir Edward Newenham, 20 July 1788; Sage, *ibid.*, page 251.

James Madison

Constitution as "a compact or treaty"[8] between "the people of the several States."[9] In a letter to General Henry Knox, dated 17 June 1788, he wrote, "I can not but hope that the States which may be disposed to make a secession [from the Union] will think often and seriously on the consequence."[10] Eleven days later, writing to General Pinckney, he announced that New Hampshire had "acceded to the new Confederacy," and, referring to North Carolina, he said, "I should be astonished if that State should withdraw from the Union."[11]

James Madison, who is commonly referred to as "the father of the Constitution," and who was in an authoritative position to properly interpret that instrument, envisioned a "confederate republic" composed of "confederate States," and described the proposed constitutional system as "a confederacy founded on republican principles, and composed of republican members."[12] He was certainly aware of the "republican principles" contained in the Declaration of Independence which stated, not only that gov-

---

8. Washington to David Stuart, 17 October 1787; Sage, *ibid.*, page 247.

9. Washington to Count Rochambeau, 8 January 1788; Sage, *ibid.*, page 248.

10. Washington to Henry Knox, 17 June 1788; Sage, *ibid.*, pages 249-250.

11. Washington to Pinckney, 28 June 1788; Sage, *ibid.*, page 250.

12. *Federalist Papers*, Number XLIII.

ernments are not republican which do not "deriv[e] their just powers from the consent of the governed," but that, should a government not answer to the purposes for which it was established, "it is the right of the people to alter or to abolish it, and to institute new government, laying its foundation on such principles and organizing its powers in such form, as to them shall seem most likely to effect their safety and happiness." Indeed, practically repeating the words of Thomas Jefferson in the Declaration of Independence, he wrote of "the great principle of self-preservation" and of "the transcendent law of nature and of nature's God, which declares that the safety and happiness of society are the objects at which all political institutions aim, and to which all such institutions must be sacrificed."[13]

Madison also said, "Were the plan of the Convention adverse to the public happiness, my voice would be, Reject the plan. Were the Union itself inconsistent with the public happiness, it would be, Abolish the Union."[14] It may be argued that these were Madison's opinions *prior* to ratification of the Constitution and therefore cannot be made to apply to the status of the States *after* they had entered the new Union. However, as late as 1830, after the new system had been operational for over forty years, he was still uncertain "whether the Union will answer the ends of its existence or otherwise." He went on:

---

13. *Ibid.*

14. *Ibid.*, Number XLV.

Should the provisions of the Constitution as here reviewed be found not to secure the Government and rights of the States against usurpations and abuses on the part of the United States, the final resort within the purview of the Constitution lies in an amendment of the Constitution according to a process applicable by the States.

And in the event of a failure of every constitutional resort, and an accumulation of usurpations and abuses, rendering passive obedience and nonresistance a greater evil than resistance and revolution, there can remain but one resort, the last of all, an appeal from the cancelled obligations of the constitutional compact, to original rights and the law of self-preservation. This is the *ultima ratio* under all Government, whether consolidated, confederated, or a compound of both; and it cannot be doubted that a single member of the Union, in the extremity supposed, but in that only, would have a right, as an extra and ultra constitutional right, to make the appeal.[15]

This was not the first time that Madison had described the Union in terms of a compact between the States. In a speech delivered before the Virginia Legislature in December of 1798, he said, "The Constitution of the United States was formed by the sanction of the States, given by each in its sovereign

---

15. Madison to the *North American Review*, 28 August 1830; Marvin Meyers (editor), *The Mind of the Founder: Sources of the Political Thought of James Madison* (Indianapolis, Indiana: The Bobbs-Merrill Company, 1973), page 529.

capacity.... The States... [are] the parties to the constitutional compact...."[16] Twenty-three years later, his views had not changed: "Our governmental system is established by a compact, not between the Government of the United States and the State Governments, but between the States as sovereign communities, stipulating each with the other a surrender of certain portions of their respective authorities, to be exercised by a common Government, and a reservation for their own exercise, of all the other authorities."[17] In the Kentucky Resolutions of November, 1798, Thomas Jefferson described the Constitution as "this compact" to which "each State acceded as a State, and is an integral party...."[18] Similarly, Gouverneur Morris, who served on the Committee on Style which delivered the final wording of the Constitution, stated that his purpose in attending the Convention of 1787 was "to form a compact for the good of America." He was "ready to do so with all the States" and, in the event that not all States would enter such a compact, he expressed his desire "to join with any States that would." In his mind, "the

---

16. George McHenry, *The Cotton Trade: Its Bearing Upon the Prosperity of Great Britain and Commerce of the American Republics* (London: Saunders, Otley, and Company, 1863), page xxxii.

17. Madison to the *North American Review*, 28 August 1830; Meyers, *Mind of the Founder*, page 529.

18. Kentucky Resolutions, 10 November 1798.

compact was to be voluntary."[19] Even Alexander Hamilton, who advocated a strong centralized government bordering on a monarchy, had to admit that the Union under the proposed Constitution would "still be, in fact and in theory, an association of States, or a confederacy."[20] Hamilton was not so dull-witted as to believe secession from a confederacy of States to be impossible, since that is precisely what each of the States would have to do in relation to the Articles of Confederation "in order to form a more perfect Union" under the Constitution.[21] In a letter to Timothy Pickering dated 16 September 1803, he wrote that, despite his disappointment with the results of the Convention, the republican form of government set forth in the Constitution "should have a fair and full trial," and then added, "I sincerely hope that it may not hereafter be discovered, that through want of sufficient attention to the last idea, the experiment of republican government, even in this country, has not been as complete, as satisfactory, and as decisive as could be wished."[22] Thus,

---

19. Speech delivered on 12 July 1787; John Scott, *The Lost Principle: How the Sectional Equilibrium Was Created, How It Was Destroyed, and How It May Be Restored* (Richmond, Virginia: James Woodhouse and Company, 1860), page 44.

20. *Federalist Papers*, Number IX.

21. George Ticknor Curtis, *History of the Origin, Formation, and Adoption of the Constitution of the United States* (New York: Harper and Brothers, 1855), Volume II, pages 181-182.

22. Max Farrand (editor), *The Records of the Federal Convention of 1787* (New Haven, Connecticut: Yale University Press,

American "republicanism" was clearly identified in the minds of these framers with sovereign States in voluntary union, or, more accurately, confederation with one another.

It is interesting to note that State sovereignty and the reserved right of secession was taught by the United States Government to cadets at West Point Military Academy during the 1825-1826 term, and perhaps longer, through William Rawle's book, *A View of the Constitution of the United States of America*.[23] In this book, which was also used as a political textbook by several other colleges and academies throughout the country at the time,[24] the author, a Philadelphia lawyer and staunch Federalist, wrote the following:

> It depends on the state itself to retain or abolish the principle of representation, because it de-

---

1911), Volume III, page 398.

23. Edgar S. Dudley, "Was 'Secession' Taught at West Point?", *The Century Magazine* (New York, 1909), Volume LXXVIII, page 635. In his biography of Robert E. Lee, Douglas Southall Freeman mentioned the tradition that Rawle's book was used at West Point beyond 1826 (*R.E. Lee: A Biography* [New York: Charles Scribner's Sons, 1935], Volume I, page 79). For example, Dabney H. Maury, who graduated in 1846, claimed that the book was used at West Point as late as 1861 ("West Point and Secession," *Southern Historical Society Papers* 6 [July-Dec., 1878], page 249).

24. *The National Cyclopedia of American Biography* (New York: James T. White and Company, 1897), Volume VII, page 442.

pends on itself whether it will continue a member of the Union. To deny this right would be inconsistent with the principle of which all our political systems are founded, which is, that the people have in all cases, a right to determine how they will be governed....

The secession of a state from the Union depends on the will of the people of such state. The people alone, as we have already seen, hold the power to alter their constitutions. But in any manner by which a secession is to take place, nothing is more certain than that the act should be deliberate, clear, and unequivocal. To withdraw from the Union is a solemn, serious act. Whenever it may appear expedient to the people of a state, it must be manifested in a direct and unequivocal manner.[25]

---

25. William Rawle, *A View of the Constitution of United States of America* (Philadelphia, Pennsylvania: Philip H. Nicklin and Company, 1829), pages 296, 302.

CHAPTER TWO
Joseph Story's Theory
of a Consolidated Nation

It is clear from the available historical facts that the Constitution would have never been ratified if it had been understood that, in doing so, the States would surrender their sovereignty, as well as their right of secession should the experiment fail. We need look no further for proof of the reserved right of secession than in the ratification of at least three of the original thirteen States. Following are excerpts from the ratifications of the States of Virginia, New York, and Rhode Island respectively:

> We, the delegates of the people of Virginia, duly elected in pursuance of a recommendation from the general assembly, and now met in convention, having fully and freely investigated and discussed the proceedings of the Federal Convention, and being prepared as well as the most mature deliberation hath enabled us to decide thereon, Do, in the name and in behalf of the people of Virginia, declare and make known that the powers granted

under the Constitution being derived from the people of the United States may be resumed by them whensoever the same shall be perverted to their injury or oppression, and that every power not granted thereby remains with them and at their will.... That each State in the Union shall, respectively, retain every power, jurisdiction and right which is not by this Constitution delegated to the Congress of the United States, or to the Departments of the Federal Government.[1]

We, the delegates of the people of New York... do declare and make known that the powers of government may be reassumed by the people whenever it shall become necessary to their happiness; that every power, jurisdiction, and right which is not by the said Constitution clearly delegated to the Congress of the United States, or the department of the government thereof, remains to the people of the several States, or to their respective State governments, to whom they may have granted the same; and that those clauses in the said Constitution, which declare that Congress shall not have or exercise certain powers, do not imply that Congress is entitled to any powers not given by the said Constitution; but such clauses are to be construed either as exceptions in certain specified pow-

---

1. Virginia Ordinance of Ratification, 25 June 1788; Jonathan Elliott, *The Debates in the Several State Conventions on the Adoption of the Federal Constitution* (Washington, D.C.: self-published, 1837), Volume V, page 3.

ers or as inserted merely for greater caution.[2]

We, the delegates of the people of Rhode Island and Plantations, duly elected... do declare and make known... that the powers of government may be resumed by the people whenever it shall become necessary to their happiness; that every power, jurisdiction, and right which is not by the said Constitution clearly delegated to the Congress of the United States, or the department of the government thereof, remains to the people of the several States, or to their respective State governments, to whom they may have granted the same;... that the United States shall guarantee to each State its sovereignty, freedom, and independence, and every power, jurisdiction, and right, which is not by this Constitution expressly delegated to the United States.[3]

The importance of these statements was explained by Jefferson Davis:

These expressions are not mere *obiter dicta*, thrown out incidentally, and entitled only to be regarded as an expression of opinion by their authors. Even if only such, they would carry great weight as the deliberately expressed judgment of enlightened contemporaries; but they are more: they

---

2. New York Ordinance of Ratification; in *Documentary History of the United States Constitution* (Washington, D.C.: U.S. Department of State, 1894), Volume II, page 191.

3. Rhode Island Ordinance of Ratification; *ibid.*, Volume II, page 311, 316.

are parts of the very acts or ordinances by which
these States ratified the Constitution and acceded
to the Union, and can not be detached from them.
If they are invalid, the ratification itself was invalid,
for they are inseparable. By inserting these declarations in their ordinances, Virginia, New York, and
Rhode Island, formally, officially, and permanently,
declared their interpretation of the Constitution as
recognizing the right of secession by the resump-
tion of their grants. By accepting the ratifications
with this declaration incorporated, the other States
as formally accepted the principle which it asserted.[4]

It was not until the Nineteenth Century was
well underway that the theory of a permanently consolidated nation from which withdrawal was unlaw-
ful first made an appearance in Joseph Story's *Commentaries on the Constitution*.[5] Daniel Webster
would rely heavily on this theory in his debates in
Congress, first with South Carolina Senator Robert
Hayne in 1830 and then with John C. Calhoun, also
of South Carolina, three years later. The proponents
of this novel theory denied that the Constitution was
either "a compact between State governments" or
that it had been "established by the people of the
several States," asserting that it had instead been es-

---

4. Jefferson Davis, *The Rise and Fall of the Confederate Government* (New York: D. Appleton and Company, 1881), Volume I, page 173.

5. Joseph Story, *Commentaries on the Constitution* (Boston:
Hilliard, Gray and Company, 1833).

Joseph Story

tablished by "the people of the United States in the aggregate."[6] The States had thus never been sovereign political bodies, for they were the creatures of the Union rather than *vice versa*. Therefore, it was reasoned, for the people of a State to declare their independence from this indivisible Union was to declare the impossible and to commit an act of treason against the nation which had given it the right to exist. In the words of Webster:

> This word "accede," not found either in the Constitution itself or in the ratification of it by any one of the States, has been chosen for use here, doubtless not without a well-considered purpose. The natural converse of accession is secession; and therefore, when it is stated that the people of the States acceded to the Union, it may be more plausibly argued that they may secede from it. If, in adopting the Constitution, nothing was done but acceding to a compact, nothing would seem necessary, in order to break it up, but to secede from the

---

6. Thomas Hart Benton (editor), *Abridgment of the Debates of Congress 1789 to 1856* (New York: D. Appleton and Company, 1857), Volume X, page 448. With this assertion, Webster contradicted his earlier, and correct, assertions in an 1819 address to Congress, not only that the States enjoyed "the exclusive possession of sovereignty" within their own boundaries, but that "the only parties to the Constitution, contemplated by it originally, were the thirteen confederated States" and that the Constitution "rests on compact" (*A Memorial to the Congress of the United States on the Subject of Restraining the Increase of Slavery in New States to be Admitted Into the Union* [Boston: Sewell Phelps, 1819], page 7).

same compact. But the term is wholly out of place. Accession, as a word applied to political associations, implies coming into a league, treaty, or confederacy, by one hitherto a stranger to it; and secession implies departing from such league or confederacy. The people of the United States have used no such form of expression in establishing the present Government.... There is no language in the whole Constitution applicable to a confederation of States. In the Constitution it is the people who speak, not the States.[7]

A review of the writings of Washington, Madison, and the other framers, including even Hamilton, will show that these men were not at all shy in using the very terms which Webster decried as "wholly out of place" when describing the nature of the Federal Union under the Constitution. According to the very men directly involved in its creation, the Constitution was a compact to which each State, acting upon its own authority, voluntarily acceded. Therefore, secession of a State from the Union, though undesirable, was nevertheless a possibility. What is most remarkable about the opposite theory is that it originated from within the rapidly dwindling ranks of the old Federalist party, which had been, less than a generation before, the chief agitator for the secession of the Northeastern States from the Union. Having been driven from power by the elec-

---

7. Benton, *Abridgement of the Debates of Congress*, Volume IX, Part I, pages 556, 566.

tion of Thomas Jefferson in 1800, the Federalists were thereafter, during the second war with England, seen agitating once again for the secession of those States and for the establishment of a New England confederacy. Story's own State of Massachusetts was the most vocal in proclaiming the doctrine of State sovereignty and the right of nullification which would later be so ably championed by Calhoun and so vehemently opposed by Story's apprentice, Webster.

As a Supreme Court justice, Story "perpetually insisted on construing the Constitution from the standpoint of that small and defeated party in the Federal Convention which wanted to form a government on the model of the English monarchy in everything but the name."[8] This was the party which, while John Adams was President, was responsible for passing the Alien and Sedition Acts of 1796, the latter of which prescribed a two thousand dollar fine and two years imprisonment for anyone who "should write or publish, or cause to be published, any libel against the Government of the United States, or either House of Congress, or against the President." C. Chauncey Burr described the effects of this Act: "A great many editors, and other gentlemen, were imprisoned under this act. Even to ridicule the President was pronounced by the corrupt partisan judges

---

8. C. Chauncey Burr, "Introduction," in Abel P. Upshur, *The True Nature and Character of Our Federal Government* (New York: Van Evrie, Horton and Company, [1840] 1868), page i.

a violation of the law. Men were beaten almost to death for neglecting to pull off their hats when the President was passing, and every man who did not instantly prostrate himself before the ensigns of Federal royalty, was denounced as the enemy of his country."[9] Both the Alien and Sedition Acts were promptly denounced by Thomas Jefferson in the Kentucky Resolutions and by James Madison in the Virginia Resolutions, and they were thereafter repealed. The Federalists not long afterwards violated the spirit of their own sedition law in the deprecations they heaped upon the Government, and the President in particular, during the War of 1812.[10]

Had Alexander Hamilton, the consummate monarchist at the Constitutional Convention of 1787, still been living when Story's *Commentaries* were initially published in 1833, they would have likely received his hearty endorsement. Unfortunately, due to their otherwise brilliant content, they did not receive the reprobation they deserved for their advancement of the consolidationist heresy of the Federalists, and they soon supplanted the abler work of Story's more honest Federalist colleague, William Rawle, as the textbook most widely consulted by politicians and lawyers on questions of American constitutional law.

It should be noted that in 1833, the records of

---

9. Burr, in Upshur, *ibid.*, page iii.

10. Matthew Carey, *The Olive Branch* (Philadelphia, Pennsylvania: M. Carey and Son, 1818).

the debates in the Philadelphia Convention had not yet been published and since the proceedings had been conducted in secret, their contents were entirely unknown to the public. Furthermore, the generation of men who had participated in the founding of the Republic under the Constitution, with but one exception, had passed from the scene when Story's theory appeared on the political stage.[11] Had a Jefferson or even a Washington still lived to rebut Story's postulations, it is doubtful that his work would have long survived or risen above obscurity.[12]

In 1840, Abel P. Upshur, a lawyer from Virginia who served as Secretary of the Navy in the Tyler Administration, published his brilliant response to Story entitled *The True Nature and Character of Our Federal Government*. Responding to Story's

---

11. James Madison was the last surviving member of the Convention of 1787, dying in 1836 at the age of 85.

12. Madison had appointed a thirty-two year old Story to the Supreme Court in 1811. At that time, Story's understanding of the nature of the Union was similar to Madison's and it was hoped that his presence on the Court would serve as a check to the nationalist views of Chief Justice John Marshall. Marshall had been appointed to the Court a decade earlier by the then-exiting second President, John Adams, whose administration had come under intense criticism for its brazen attempts to expand Federal power through the Alien and Sedition acts of 1798. Even though the Federalist party was vanquished with the election of Jefferson to the Presidency, the tendency to strengthen Federal power at the expense of the States survived in the judicial tenure of Marshall, and had a profound influence on Story's own views to turn them in a nationalistic direction.

claim that, prior to the severance of political ties with Great Britain, the people of the thirteen colonies "were in a strict sense fellow-subjects, and in a variety of respects, one people," Upshur wrote:

> In order to constitute "one people," in a political sense, of the inhabitants of different countries, something more is necessary than that they should owe a common allegiance to a common sovereign.... By the term "people," as here used, we do not mean merely a number of persons. We mean by it a political corporation, the members of which owe a common allegiance to a common sovereignty, and do not owe any allegiance which is *not* common; who are bound by no laws except such as that sovereignty may prescribe; who owe to one another reciprocal obligations; who possess common political interests; who are liable to common political duties; and who can exert no sovereign power except in the name of the whole. Anything short of this, would be an imperfect definition of that political corporation which we call "a people."
>
> Tested by this definition, the people of the American colonies were, in no conceivable sense, "one people." They owed, indeed, allegiance to the British King, as the head of each colonial government, and as forming a part thereof; but this allegiance was exclusive, in each colony, to its own government, and, consequently, to the King as the head thereof and was not a common allegiance of the people of all the colonies, to a common head. These colonial governments were clothed with the sovereign power of making laws, and of enforcing

obedience to them, from their own people. The people of one colony owed no allegiance to the government of any other colony, and were not bound by its laws. The colonies had no common legislature, no common treasury, no common military power, no common judicatory. The people of one colony were not liable to pay taxes to any other colony, nor to bear arms in its defence; they had no right to vote in its elections; no influence nor control in its municipal government; no interest in its municipal institutions. There was no prescribed form by which the colonies could act together, for any purpose whatever; they were not known as "one people" in any one function of government. Although they were all, alike, dependencies of the British Crown, yet, even in the action of the parent country, in regard to them, they were recognized as separate and distinct. They were established at different times, and each under an authority from the Crown, which applied to itself alone. They were not even alike in their organization. Some were provincial, some proprietary, and some charter governments. Each derived its form of government from the particular instrument establishing it, or from assumptions of power acquiesced in by the Crown, without any connection with, or relation to, any other. They stood upon the same footing, in every respect, with other British colonies, with nothing to distinguish their relation either to the parent country or to one another (emphasis in original).[13]

---

13. Upshur, *ibid*., pages 22-23.

Referring to the Declaration of Independence, Judson A. Landon wrote, "The thought in the mind of the framers no doubt was that every colony was free and independent of the king. There was no need to say independent of each other; they had always been so, and the idea of erecting a common, central government out of all, was not yet suggested."[14] That this was how the signers of the Declaration understood their own political condition is beyond dispute. For example, while separation from Great Britain was still being discussed, James Wilson noted, "All the different members of the British empire are distinct states, independent of each other, but connected together under the same sovereign."[15] Samuel Chase, another signer of the Declaration who later served on the Supreme Court during Washington's administration, likewise attested to the fact that the former "united colonies" were "each of them... a sovereign and independent state, that is, that each of them had a right to govern itself by its own authority and its own laws, without any control from any other power on earth."[16] These statements undermine Story's supposition that the Declaration of Independence necessarily consolidated the inhabitants of the former col-

_____

14. Judson A. Landon, *The Constitutional History and Government of the United States* (Boston: Houghton, Mifflin and Company, 1905), page 59.

15. T.R. Fehrenbach, *Greatness to Spare* (Princeton, New Jersey: D. Van Nostrand, 1968), page 107.

16. *Ware v. Hylton* (1796), 3 Dallas 224.

onies into "one people." According to Story, "The colonies did not severally act for themselves, and proclaim their own independence."[17] Not only is this assertion proven false by the very words of the Declaration itself, which, in its closing paragraph, referred to the colonies as possessing the right "to be Free and Independent States," but also by the Treaty of Peace, signed at Paris on 3 September 1783, in which King George III acknowledged, separately and by name, each of the thirteen former colonies "to be free sovereign and independent states," promising to "treat with them as such." Upshur wrote:

> The Congress of 1775, by which independence was declared, was appointed... by the colonies in their separate and distinct capacity, each acting for itself, and not conjointly with any other. They were the representatives each of his own colony, and not of any other; each had authority to act in the name of his own colony, and not in that of any other; each colony gave its own vote by its own representatives, and not by those of any other colony. Of course, it was as separate and distinct colonies that they deliberated on the Declaration of Independence. When, therefore, they declare, in the adoption of that measure, that they act as "the representatives of the United States of America," and "in the name and by the authority of the good people of these colonies," they must of course be understood as speaking in the character of which they

17. Story, *Commentaries on the Constitution*, Volume I, page 197.

had all along acted; that is, as the representatives of separate and distinct colonies, and not as the joint representatives of any one people.... It is impossible to suppose, therefore, in common justice to the sagacity of Congress, that they meant anything more by the Declaration of Independence, than simply to sever the tie which had theretofore bound them to England, and to assert the rights of the separate and distinct colonies, as separate and independent States; particularly as the language which they use is fairly susceptible of this construction. The instrument itself is entitled, "The Unanimous Declaration of the Thirteen United States of America;" of *States*, separate and distinct bodies politic, and not of "one people" or nation, composed of all of them together; "united," as independent States may be, by compact or agreement, and not *amalgamated*, as they would be, if they formed *one* nation or body politic (emphasis in original).[18]

While the colonies were certainly united militarily in their efforts to throw off the yoke of British tyranny, they had no such political union as envisioned by Story. On this point, all constitutional authorities prior to Story were agreed. According to Thomas M. Cooley, "At the opening of their struggle for Independence the American States had no common bond of union except such as exist in a common cause and common danger. They were not yet a nation; they were only a loose Confederacy; no compact or articles of agreement determined the duties of

---

18. Upshur, *Our Federal Government*, pages 53-55.

the several members to each other, or to the confederacy as an aggregate of all."[19] In discussing the origin of American institutions, James Monroe noted two indisputable facts: "The first is, that in wresting the power, or what is called the sovereignty, from the crown, it passed directly to the people. The second, that it passed directly to the people of each colony, and not to the people of all the colonies in the aggregate; to thirteen distinct communities, and not to one."[20] There would be no real political union between the fledgling States until they became so associated under the Articles of Confederation, and even then, we find in the second article of that document the declaration that each State "retains its sovereignty, freedom, and independence, and every power, jurisdiction, and right which is not by this Confederation expressly delegated to the United States in Congress assembled." Obviously, then, when Jefferson in the Declaration spoke of a time when "it becomes necessary for one people to dissolve the political bands which have connected them them with another, and to assume among the powers of the earth, the separate and equal station to which the laws of Nature and of Nature's God entitle them," he was either speaking abstractly or applying the phrase "one people" to each of the colonies re-

---

19. Thomas M. Cooley, *Michigan: A History of Governments* (Boston: Houghton, Mifflin and Company, 1895), page 120.

20. Paper transmitted to Congress, May 4, 1822; Hezekiah Niles, *Nile's Weekly Register* (Baltimore, Maryland: William Ogden Niles, 1822), Volume XXII, page 366.

spectively. Read in any other way, the Declaration would place Jefferson, the champion of decentralization and of State sovereignty, squarely in the camp of Hamilton, the consolidationist. The absurdity of such an attempt is too transparent for comment.

Finally, Story brought his faulty premise to an equally faulty conclusion: the "one people" who issue their Declaration of Independence in 1776 are the same "people of the United States" who, in 1787 "do ordain and establish this Constitution for the United States of America." Thus, the theory of the people "in the aggregate" is presented for our consideration. However, Story fared no better in his exposition of this doctrine than in his exposition of those preceding it, for his thesis is immediately disproved when the original wording of the Preamble is read: "We, the people of the States of New Hampshire, Massachusetts, Rhode Island and Providence Plantations, Connecticut, New York, New Jersey, Pennsylvania, Delaware, Maryland, Virginia, North Carolina, South Carolina and Georgia, do ordain, declare and establish the following Constitution, for the government of ourselves and our posterity."[21]

Upshur commented:

> On the very next day this preamble was unanimously adopted; and the reader will at once perceive, that it carefully preserves the distinct sov-

---

21. Jonathan Elliott (editor), *Journal and Debates of the Federal Convention* (Washington, D.C.: self-published, 1836), Volume I, page 255.

ereignty of the States, and discountenances all idea of consolidation. The draft of the Constitution thus submitted was discussed, and various alterations and amendments adopted (but without any change in the preamble), until the 8th of September, 1787, when the following resolution was passed: "It was moved and seconded to appoint a committee of five, to revise the style of, and arrange the articles agreed to by, the House; which passed in the affirmative." It is manifest that this committee had no power to change the *meaning* of anything which had been adopted, but were authorized merely to "revise the style," and arrange the matter in proper order. On the 12th of the same month they made their report. The preamble, as they reported it, is in the following words: "We, *the people of the United States*, in order to form a more perfect union...." It does not appear that any attempt was made to change this phraseology in any material point, or to reinstate the original. The presumption is, therefore, that the two were considered as substantially the same, particularly as the committee had no authority to make any change except in the style....

There is, however, another and a perfectly conclusive reason for the change of phraseology, from the States by name, to the more general expression "the United States;" and this, too, without supposing that it was intended thereby to convey a different idea as to the parties of the Constitution. The revised draft contained a proviso, that the Constitution should go into operation when adopted and ratified by nine States. It was, of course, uncertain whether more than nine would adopt it or not, and if they should not, it would be altogether improper to name them as parties to that instrument (emphasis in original).[22]

The testimony of the framers themselves substantiate Upshur's observations. In response to Patrick Henry's fear that what was being established by the Constitution "must be one great consolidated national government of the people of all the States"[23] – Story's theory of the people in the aggregate – James Madison said:

Who are parties to it? The people – but not the people as composing one great body; but the people as composing thirteen sovereignties: were it, as the gentleman [Henry] asserts, a consolidated government, the assent of a majority of the people would be sufficient for its establishment, and as a majority have adopted it already, the remaining States would be bound by the act of the majority, even if they unanimously reprobated it: were it such a government as is suggested, it would be now binding on the people of this State [Virginia], without having had the privilege of deliberating upon it; but, sir, no State is bound by it, as it is, without its own consent. Should all the States adopt it, it will be then a government established by the thirteen States of America, not through the intervention of the Legislatures, but by the people at large. In this particular respect the distinction between the exist-

---

22. Upshur, *Our Federal Government*, pages 70-72.
23. Elliott, *Journal and Debates*, Volume III, page 54.

ing and proposed governments is very material. The existing system has been derived from the dependent, derivative authority of the Legislatures of the States, whereas this is derived from the superior power of the people.[24]

Elsewhere, Madison added:

The Constitution is to be founded on the assent and ratification of the people of America, given by deputies elected for the special purpose; but this assent and ratification is to be given by the people, not as individuals comprising one entire nation, but as composing the distinct and independent States to which they respectively belong. It is to be the assent and ratification of the several States, derived from the supreme authority in each State – the authority of the people themselves. The act, therefore, establishing the Constitution will not be a *national*, but a *federal* act.

That it will be a federal, and not a national act, as these terms are understood by objectors, the act of the people, as forming so many independent States, not as forming one aggregate nation, is obvious from this single consideration, that it is to result neither from the decision of a *majority* of the people of the Union, nor from that of a *majority* of the States. It must result from the *unanimous* assent of the several States that are parties to it, differing no otherwise from their ordinary assent than in its being expressed, not by the legislative authority, but by that of the people themselves. Were the peo-

24. Elliott, *ibid.*, pages 114-115.

ple regarded in this transaction as forming one nation, the will of the majority of the whole people of the United States would bind the minority; in the same manner as the majority in each State must bind the minority; and the will of the majority must be determined either by a comparison of the individual votes, or by considering the will of the majority of the States, as evidences of the will of a majority of the people of the United States. Neither of these has been adopted. Each State, in ratifying the Constitution, is considered as a sovereign body, independent of all others, and only to be bound by its voluntary act (emphasis in original).[25]

Likewise, Luther Martin, one of the delegates to the Philadelphia Convention in 1787, commented:

At the separation from the British Empire, the people of America preferred the establishment of themselves into thirteen separate sovereignties instead of incorporating themselves into one: to these they look up for the security of their lives, liberties and properties: to these they must look up. The federal government they formed, to defend the whole against foreign nations, in case of war, and to defend the lesser States against the ambition of the larger: they are afraid of granting powers unnecessarily, lest they should defeat the original end of the Union; lest the powers should prove dangerous to the sovereignties of the particular States

---

25. *Federalist Papers*, Number XXXIX.

which the Union was meant to support....[26]

William Patterson, another delegate who later became Governor of New Jersey, had this to say of the intent of the Convention:

> Can we, on this ground, form a national Government? I fancy not. Our commissions give a complexion to the business; and can we suppose that, when we exceed the bounds of our duty, the people will approve our proceedings?
>
> We are met here as the deputies of thirteen independent, sovereign States, for federal purposes. Can we consolidate their sovereignty and form one nation, and annihilate the sovereignties of our States, who have sent us here for other purposes?[27]

Such statements as these are to be found in abundance throughout the writings, public statements, and private correspondence of the men living at the time of the adoption of the Constitution, especially those who were instrumental in the actual framing of the document. Since Story and Webster had access to many of these writings, especially the *Federalist Papers*, one is left to conclude that their groundless theories and postulations were the product of a deliberate and pre-meditated attempt to deceive their followers.

---

26. Speech delivered on 20 June 1787; Madison, *Debates in the Federal Convention*, Volume I, page 205.

27. Madison, *ibid*., page 76.

CHAPTER THREE
Abraham Lincoln Resurrects the Monarchical Theory

It was the demonstrably false monarchical theory of Story and Webster which Abraham Lincoln, contrary to the intent of the framers of the Constitution, contrary to the disunionist sentiments of prominent members of the Republican party,[1] and contrary even to the pro-secession views expressed at one time by himself on the floor of Congress,[2]

---

1. See statements in Chapter Four.

2. Let the reader consider the words of Lincoln himself:

> Any people anywhere, being inclined and having the power, have the right to rise up and shake off the existing government, and form a new one that suits them better. This is a most valuable, a most sacred right – a right which we hope and believe is to liberate the world. Nor is this right confined to cases in which the whole people of an existing government may choose to exercise it. Any portion of such people, that can, may revolutionize, and make their own of so much of the territory as they inhabit (speech delivered in the U.S. House of Representatives on 12 January 1848; *Con-*

adopted and proclaimed in his first Inaugural Address of 4 March 1861:

> I hold that in contemplation of universal law and of the Constitution the Union of these States is perpetual. Perpetuity is implied, if not expressed, in the fundamental law of all national governments. It is safe to assert that no government proper ever had a provision in its organic law for its own termination. Continue to execute all the express provisions of our National Constitution, and the Union will endure forever, it being impossible to destroy it except by some action not provided for in the instrument itself....
>
> Descending from these general principles, we find the proposition that in legal contemplation

---

gressional Globe, Volume XIX, page 94).

Technically, Lincoln was referring to the "right of revolution" stated in the Declaration of Independence rather than the right of a State under the Constitution to secede from the Union. This was just one of the many times he displayed his penchant for inconsistency. If the thirteen colonies had a right to separate from the British Crown to whom they were *subject*, why did not the thirteen Southern States have the right to peacefully withdraw from their sister States with whom they were *co-equals*? If the political condition of the States in 1861 was more mature than it had been in 1776, then so was their right of separation. If the natural right of separation existed under the royal charters which gave them existence, then it also existed under a Constitution which they, by an act of their sovereign ratification, had brought into existence. The logic is inescapable even though it was later lost on Lincoln when he became President.

the Union is perpetual confirmed by the history of the Union itself. The Union is much older than the Constitution. It was formed, in fact, by the Articles of Association in 1774. It was matured and continued by the Declaration of Independence in 1776. It was further matured, and the faith of all the then thirteen States expressly plighted and engaged that it should be perpetual, by the Articles of Confederation in 1778 [sic]. And finally, in 1787, one of the declared objects for ordaining and establishing the Constitution was "to form a more perfect Union." But if destruction of the Union by one or by a part only of the States be lawfully possible, the Union is less perfect than before the Constitution, having lost the vital element of perpetuity.

It follows from these views that no State upon its own mere motion can lawfully get out of the Union; that resolves and ordinances to that effect are legally void, and that acts of violence within any State or States against the authority of the United States are insurrectionary or revolutionary, according to circumstances.

I therefore consider that in view of the Constitution and the laws the Union is unbroken, and to the extent of my ability, I shall take care, as the Constitution itself expressly enjoins upon me, that the laws of the Union be faithfully executed in all the States. Doing this I deem to be only a simple duty on my part, and I shall perform it so far as practicable unless my rightful masters, the American people, shall withhold the requisite means or in some authoritative manner direct the contrary. I trust this will not be regarded as a men-

Abraham Lincoln

ace, but only as the declared purpose of the Union that it will constitutionally defend and maintain itself.[3]

Lincoln elaborated on this view in his address to Congress in special session on 4 July 1861:

> Our States have neither more nor less power than that reserved to them in the Union by the Constitution, no one of them ever having been a State *out* of the Union.... Having never been States, either in substance or in name, *outside* the Union, whence this magical omnipotence of "State rights," asserting a claim of power to lawfully destroy the Union itself? Much is said about the "sovereignty" of the States, but the word even is not in the National Constitution, nor, as is believed, in any of the State constitutions.... The States have their status in the Union, and they have no other legal status. If they break from this, they can do so only against law and by revolution. The Union, and not themselves separately, procured their independence and their liberty. By conquest or purchase the Union gave each of them whatever of independence and liberty it has. The Union is older than the States, and, in fact, it created them as States (emphasis in original).[4]

---

3. *Inaugural Addresses of the Presidents of the United States From George Washington to George Bush* (Washington, D.C.: Government Printing Office, 1989).

4. James D. Richardson (editor), *A Compilation of the Messages and Papers of the Presidents* (Washington, D.C.: Bureau of National Literature, 1922), Volume VII, page 3228.

Lincoln, the small town lawyer, had either not done his homework or had chosen to ignore the clear testimony of the historical record. It was his assertion that no State had "been a State *out* of the Union... either in substance or in name." However, the States of North Carolina and Rhode Island were indeed, both "in substance and in name," out of the Union after the Constitution had already been in operation for, in the case of the former, nearly nine months, and in the case of the latter, a full fifteen months. It was hoped that both States would eventually ratify the Constitution and thus accede to the Union thereunder, but no one suggested that either North Carolina or Rhode Island should be treated by the eleven States of the then-existing Federal Union as anything less than sovereign political bodies. For example, George Washington, in his capacity as President of the United States, wrote to the Senate on 26 September 1789: "Having yesterday received a letter written in this month by the Governor of Rhode Island, at the request and in behalf of the General Assembly of that State, addressed to the President, the Senate, and the House of Representatives of the eleven United States of America in Congress assembled, I take the earliest opportunity of laying a copy of it before you."[5] Portions of the letter mentioned by Washington follow:

---

5. This document appears under the title "Rhode Island desires to maintain friendly relations with the United States" in *American State Papers: Miscellaneous* (Document 207), Volume I, page 9.

State of Rhode Island and Providence Plantations, In General Assembly, September Session, 1789.

To the President, the Senate, and the House of Representatives of the eleven United States of America in Congress assembled:

The critical situation in which the people of this State are placed engages us to make these assurances, on their behalf, of their attachment and friendship to their sister States, and of their disposition to cultivate mutual harmony and friendly intercourse. They know themselves to be a handful, comparatively viewed, and, although they now stand as it were alone, they have not separated themselves or departed from the principles of that Confederation, which was formed by the sister States in their struggle for freedom and in the hour of danger....

Our not having acceded to or adopted the new system of government formed and adopted by most of our sister States, we doubt not, has given uneasiness to them. That we have not seen our way clear to it, consistently with our idea of the principles upon which we all embarked together, has also given pain to us. We have not doubted that we might thereby avoid present difficulties, but we have apprehended future mischief....

Can it be thought strange that, with these impressions, they should wait to see the proposed system organized and in operation? – to see what further checks and securities would be agreed to and established by way of amendments, before they could adopt it as a constitution of government for themselves and their posterity?...

We are induced to hope that we shall not be altogether considered as foreigners having no particular affinity or connection with the United States; but that trade and commerce, upon which the prosperity of this State much depends, will be preserved as free and open between this State and the United States, as our different situations at present can possibly admit....

We feel ourselves attached by the strongest ties of friendship, kindred, and interest, to our sister States; and we can not, without the greatest reluctance, look to any other quarter for those advantages of commercial intercourse which we conceive to be more natural and reciprocal between them and us.

I am, at the request and in behalf of the General Assembly, your most obedient, humble servant.

John Collins, Governor[6]

In the *Federalist* Number XLIII, Madison had raised the question, "What relation is to subsist between the nine or more States ratifying the Constitution, and the remaining few who do not become parties to it?" The above letter certainly supplied the answer. It could not be clearer to the unbiased reader that it was both unabashedly declared by Governor Collins and accepted without question by the authorities of the eleven United States of America, that, not only did Rhode Island have a lawfully functioning

6. *Ibid.*, page 10.

government prior to its entrance into the Union under the Constitution, but, as a sovereign State, it was also in all respects foreign to the United States. We have already seen how the people of Rhode Island clung tenaciously to and without equivocation declared their sovereignty in their ratification of the Constitution in May of 1790, which, incidentally, was passed by a mere majority of two votes.

Lincoln's claim that the States were never acknowledged in their constitutions as sovereign is also easily disproved. The original constitution of Massachusetts opened with these words: "The people inhabiting the territory formerly called the Province of Massachusetts Bay do hereby solemnly and mutually agree with each other to form themselves into a free, sovereign, and independent body politic, or State, by the name of The Commonwealth of Massachusetts." It was this attribute of sovereignty which was boldly asserted when Massachusetts repeatedly threatened to secede from the Union.[7] The New Hampshire con-

---

7. Most Americans associate secession only with the South in the mid-Nineteenth Century, but what is not widely known is that Northern Federalists were the first to threaten to secede when the ratification of the Constitution apparently stalled in Virginia, New York, and Rhode Island. The ink on the parchment of the Constitution was scarcely dry before many in the New England States again sought to rid themselves of union with the South. In December of 1803, Colonel Timothy Pickering, who had served as Postmaster-General, Secretary of War, and Secretary of State in the cabinet of George Washington, and as a Senator from the State of Massachusetts, was very vocal in his denunciation of the Louisiana Pur-

chase because of the disruption of the balance of power between the two sections of the country which he and many of his fellow New Englanders imagined would result. Pickering suggested as the remedy the establishment of *"a new confederacy*, exempt from the corrupt and corrupting influence and oppression of the aristocratic democrats of the South" (letter to Higginson, 24 December 1803; emphasis in original; James Henry Stark, *The Loyalists of Massachusetts and the Other Side of the American Revolution* [Boston: Self-Published, 1910], page 108), and it was his prediction that this separation between North and South would occur within the next generation.

The bill for the admission of the State of Louisiana into the Union generated still more noise from Massachusetts in 1811. Complaining that the creation of additional States from the Territory of Orleans would upset the sectional balance, Josiah Quincy boldly declared in the House of Representatives on the fourteenth of January, "If this bill passes, it is my deliberate opinion that it is virtually a dissolution of the Union; that it will free the States from their moral obligation; and as it will be the right of all, so it will be the duty of some, definitely to prepare for a separation – amicably if they can, violently if they must" (speech in the House of Representatives, 14 January 1811; Benton, *Abridgement of the Debates of Congress*, Volume IV, page 327).

Northern agitation for disunion again erupted during the second war with England from 1812-1814. Dissatisfied with the war because it interfered with commercial intercourse with Great Britain, the New England States, with Massachusetts at the head, repeatedly threatened to separate from the South by violent revolution. On 14 February 1814, a committee of the Massachusetts legislature called for a convention of the New England States to discuss the formation of the Northern Confederacy. A constitution for this proposed New England confederacy was actually drawn up and was "to go into

stitution likewise referred to the State as a "free, sovereign, and independent body politic." Of course, it was not necessary for a State to declare itself to be a sovereign power in its own constitution, for such a document was but the declared will of the people of such State, in whom the sovereignty resided. It was well understood that, in a republic, as each State was and remained, a constitution may be changed or abolished as the people see fit. Lincoln was apparently under the delusion that the States were created by their constitutions, rather than *vice versa.*

Finally, the absurdity of Lincoln's assertion that the Federal Constitution nowhere applies the attribute of sovereignty to a State should have been obvious to his audience. The Constitution did not need to explicitly refer to the several States as sovereign any more than it was necessary for the constitutions of the States to do so. This was because, in its own words, it was merely a compact entered into "between the States so ratifying the same."[8] If the States were sovereign prior to their ratification of the Constitution, then they did not somehow lose that sovereignty simply because they failed to so declare themselves in the document of their own creation. We have already discussed how the States had once and for all time identified themselves in the Declaration of Independence to be "Free and Independent

---

operation as soon as two or three States shall have adopted it."
8. Article VII.

States," and were acknowledged to be such by King George when he signed the peace treaty of 1783. In this condition, they asserted "full Power to levy War, conclude Peace, contract Alliances, establish Commerce, and to do all other Acts and Things which Independent States may of right do." It was this sovereign right to "contract alliances" that gave birth to the first Union under the Articles of Confederation in which document each State expressly reserved "its sovereignty, freedom, and independence, and every power, jurisdiction, and right which is not by this Confederation expressly delegated to the United States in Congress assembled." This reservation was repeated in the Constitution, the Tenth Amendment of which states that "the powers not delegated to the United States by the Constitution, nor prohibited by it to the States, are reserved to the States respectively, or to the people." Nowhere in this document did the States surrender any portion of their sovereignty to the new Federal Government, nor was it possible for them to have done so, since true sovereignty is not an attribute capable of division:

> Under the American theory of republican government, conventions of the people, duly elected and accredited as such, are invested with the plenary power inherent in the people of an organized and independent community, assembled in mass. In other words, they represent and exercise what is properly the *sovereignty* of the people. State Legislatures, with restricted powers, do not possess or represent sovereignty. Still less does the Congress

of a union or confederacy of States, which is by two degrees removed from the seat of sovereignty. We sometimes read or hear of "delegated sovereignty," "divided sovereignty," with other loose expressions of the same sort; but no such thing as a division or delegation of sovereignty is possible (emphasis in original).[9]

Whatever was done in establishing the Constitution of government, must have been done by sovereignty. Of course I speak of voluntary action, *i.e.* free exercise and effectuation of will. So that if any sovereignty was put in the federal pact, sovereignty must, *ex mero motu*, have divided itself. It must have exerted its will, whether it intended to divide itself, or delegate powers. When this will was exerted, the Constitution was made and established, and *the said will necessarily existed through the act.* We know, then, that it was not sovereignty, but something else that was put, *by sovereignty*, in the federal pact....

Any thinking man can see that sovereignty's exercise of its right of government is functional, and involves no change of itself, in place, nature, or right, much less does it divide and conquer itself – committing *felo de se* (emphasis in original).[10]

---

9. Davis, *Rise and Fall of the Confederate Government,* Volume I, page 99.

10. Sage, *Republic of Republics*, pages 328, 329. See also Emmerich de Vattel, *The Law of Nations: Principles of the Law of Nature Applied to the Conduct and Affairs of Nations and Sovereigns* (New York: Samuel Campbell, 1796), Book I, Chapter 1, Section 65; Francis Lieber, *Civil Liberty and Self*

Instead, what the States delegated to their common agent was power to act in certain specifically enumerated instances. Agency never involves an actual transfer of one particle of the principal's sovereignty to the agent; since the latter merely acts in behalf of and in representation of the former, a sovereign agent is an obvious contradiction in terms. In the words of the Supreme Court, "While sovereign powers are delegated to the agencies of government, sovereignty itself remains with the People, by whom and for whom, all government exists and acts."[11] Hence, we find that the articles establishing each of the three Branches of the Government begin with the words, "All legislative Powers herein granted shall be vested in a Congress of the United States" (Article I), "The executive Power shall be vested in a President of the United States of America" (Article II), and "The judicial Power of the United States, shall be vested in one supreme Court, and in such inferior Courts as Congress may from time to time ordain and establish" (Article III).

If one were inclined to use Lincoln's own logic against him, it might be argued that the Federal Government cannot be sovereign because the Constitution nowhere says that it is so. However, we need not rely upon specious syllogisms to prove our point

_____

Government (Philadelphia, Pennsylvania: J.B. Lippincott and Company, 1859), page 156.

11. *Yick Wo vs. Hopkins and Woo Lee vs. Hopkins* (1886), 118 U.S. 356.

since the historical record clearly speaks for itself. In the *Federalist*, Number XL, Madison wrote that, under the new system of government, "the States, in all un-enumerated cases, are left in the enjoyment of their sovereign and independent jurisdiction," adding that "the great principles of the Constitution proposed by the Convention may be considered less as absolutely new, than as the expansion of principles which are found in the Articles of Confederation." In Number XLIII, he described the Senate as "a palladium to the residuary sovereignty of the States" – that is, the inherent powers which the States withheld from the general Government. In Number LXXXI of the same series, Alexander Hamilton also stated, without reservation, that the attribute of sovereignty "is now enjoyed by the government of every State in the Union. Unless, therefore, there is a surrender of this immunity in the plan of the Convention, it will remain with the States...." No such surrender may be found in the Constitution, but rather the opposite is clearly declared in the Tenth Amendment.

In addition to Madison and Hamilton, we also have the united testimony of the other members of the 1787 Convention. John Dickinson, who had served as President of Delaware, and later of Pennsylvania, prior to attending the Convention, described the new system as "a confederacy of republics... in which the sovereignty of each state is represented with equal suffrage in one legislative body... and the sovereignties and people... conjointly represented in a president."[12] Gouverneur Morris, the delegate from Pennsylvania who presided over the Committee on Style which was responsible for the change in the wording of the Preamble, declared some years after the Constitution had gone into effect that it was "a compact, not between individuals, but between political societies... each enjoying sovereign power, and, of course, equal rights."[13] James Wilson, also of Pennsylvania, said that the States under the Constitution "confederate[d] anew on better principles" than under the Articles and that the resulting government was "a federal body of our own creation." He went on: "Let it be remembered that the business of the federal convention was not local, but general; not limited to the views and establishments of a single state, but co-extensive with the continent, and comprehending the views and establishments of thirteen independent sovereignties."[14]

Tench Coxe, yet another delegate from Pennsylvania, said, "Had the federal convention meant to exclude the idea of 'union,' that is, of several and separate sovereignties joining in a confederacy, they would have said, 'We, the people of America,' for

---

12. John Dickinson, *The Political Writings of John Dickinson, Esquire* (Wilmington, Delaware: Bonsol and Niles, 1801), Volume II, page 107.

13. Jared Sparks, *Life of Gouverneur Morris With Selections From His Correspondence and Miscellaneous Papers* (Boston: Gary and Bowen, 1832), Volume III, page 193.

14. Elliott, *Debates in the Several State Conventions*, Volume II, page 443.

union necessarily involves the idea of competent states, which complete consolidation excludes. But the severalty of the states is frequently recognised in the most distinct manner, in the course of the Constitution."[15]

Roger Sherman stated that "the government of the United States was instituted by a number of sovereign states for the better security of their rights, and the advancement of their interests."[16] Samuel Adams of Massachusetts, at the ratification convention of that State, boldly asserted that, "consonant with the second article" of the Articles of Confederation, each State in the new Union "retains its sovereignty, freedom, and independence, and every power... not expressly delegated to the United States."[17] These men were saying nothing different than such a noted authority on international law as Emmerich de Vattel, who wrote:

> Every nation that governs itself, under what form soever, without any dependence on foreign power, is a sovereign state....

15. Matthew Carey (editor), *The American Museum: Repository of Ancient and Modern Fugitive Pieces* (Philadelphia, Pennsylvania: Self-published, 1788),Volume III, Number 1, page 160.

16. Timothy Pitkin, *A Political and Civil History of the United States From the Year 1763 to the Close of the Administration of Washington in March 1797* (New Haven, Connecticut: Hezekiah Howe, and Durrie and Peck, 1828), Volume II, page 290.

17. Elliott, *Debates in the Several State Conventions*, Volume II, page 131.

Several sovereign and independent states may unite themselves together by a perpetual confederacy, without each in particular ceasing to be a perfect state. They will form together a federal republic: the deliberations in common will offer no violence to the sovereignty of each member, though they may, in certain aspects, put some restraint on the exercise of it, in virtue of voluntary engagements. A person does not cease to be free and independent, when he is obliged to fulfill the engagements into which he has very willingly entered.[18]

As such, there could be nothing but self-imposed forbearance to keep the people of a State from exercising said sovereignty by withdrawing from the Union which they had entered of their own volition.

Thus, Lincoln's argument against State sovereignty and the right of secession rested upon the fallacious theory of Story and Webster that the American people form one conglomerate political mass, rather than a confederation of distinct political bodies. Furthermore, he interpreted the Constitution as if it were the source of political sovereignty, with certain powers being reserved by the same to each State as a king might grant a charter to a body of subjects desiring to form a colony. In light of the massive weight of evidence against these views, it is a wonder that Lincoln was not hooted from his platform by an angry crowd justly feeling their intelligence insulted by such ignorant drivel as was delivered in his first Inaugural

---

18. Vattel, *Law of Nations*, Book I, Chapter I, Sections 4, 10.

Address. It is also no less a wonder that such nonsense was accepted by the Northern people as justification for war against the South. Bernard Janin Sage wrote:

> Would to God these perversions and blunders had been as harmless as they are amusing!... These are called "constitutional views!" If "views" at all, they are "views" *afar off* – through the moral mirage of platforms, partisan speeches, and sectional commentaries, which distort every thing, and turn it upside down. Why! if Hamilton, Jay, Washington, Hancock, Franklin, and all those fathers who were so fortunate as to die early, were to re-visit their beloved America, such "views" would astonish them as much as it would to see people standing on their heads, houses inverted, ships "walking the waters," with masts for legs; trees rooted in the sky; rivers running to their sources; or babes giving birth to their parents.
>
> They would find their voluntary union of states to have grown involuntary and indissoluble: states degraded to counties, and returned to a worse than British provincialism; and the *quondam* governmental agency, transmuted to an "absolute supremacy," and swaying the sceptre of an empire! (emphasis in original)[19]

---

19. Sage, *Republic of Republics*, pages 238-239.

CHAPTER FOUR
Sovereigns Cannot Rebel
Against Their Agent

In his book *The American Union*, which was published in Great Britain just after the start of the war, James Spence asked the following questions:

> Assuredly there is no disposition in this country to lean in favour of turmoil; but we cannot realize an act as that of rebellion or treason or piracy, simply because these names are applied to it. We are told that in the United States the people are sovereign. Here is an act committed by many millions of this sovereign people; against whom do they rebel? Can a sovereign, or a large portion of a sovereignty, be a rebel? In the usual meaning of our language rebellion is an act of the subject. Are, then, many millions of the sovereign people of the United States subjects, and to whom? Who is the monarch so supreme that in comparison even the sovereignty of the people may be termed a rebel? Is it the law? But where is the law? Assertions are not laws, nor yet ambitious theories, nor yet concep-

tions of advantage. Laws are enactments solemn, comprehensive, on known and legible record. Where, then, is the law which the States of the South have broken? And if in America the Government be merely an agent, then, as there exists no law that forbids the secession of a State, against whom or what do they rebel?[1]

These were questions which the demagogues in the North never attempted to answer before marching their troops southward to subjugate sovereign States. Oddly enough, the doctrine of State sovereignty and the right of secession was well understood by leading Republicans until they were all infected with sudden mass amnesia by Lincoln's first Inaugural Address. For example, William Seward, author of "The Irrepressible Conflict" and later Secretary of State in Lincoln's cabinet, stated, "Every man in this country, every man in Christendom, who knows anything of the philosophy of government, knows that this republic has been thus successful only by reason of the stability, strength, and greatness, of the individual States."[2]

On 9 November 1860, the editors of the New York *Herald* put these words into print: "The current

---

1. James Spence, *The American Union: Its Effect on National Character and Policy* (London: Richard Bentley and Son, 1862), pages 290-291.

2. Speech on 23 February 1855; William Bentley Fowl, *The Free Speaker: A New Collection of Pieces For Declamation Original as Well as Selected* (Boston: Self-Published, 1859), page 178.

of opinion seems to set strongly in favor of reconstruction, and leaving out the New England States. These latter are thought to be so fanatical it would be impossible there would be any peace under a Government to which they are parties."[3] Two days later, they continued: "The South has an undeniable right to secede from the Union. In the event of secession, the City of New York, the State of New Jersey, and very likely Connecticut, will separate from New England, where the black man is put on a pinnacle above the white. New York City is for the Union first, and for the gallant and chivalrous South afterwards."[4] Also on the ninth of November, Horace Greeley, editor of the Republican organ, the New York *Tribune*, expressed much the same sentiments:

> If the cotton States consider the value of the Union debatable, we maintain their perfect right to discuss it; nay, we hold with Jefferson, to the inalienable right of communities to alter or abolish forms of government that have become oppressive or injurious: and if the cotton States decide that they can do better out of the Union than in it, we insist on letting them go in peace. The right to secede may be a revolutionary one, but it exists nev-

3. New York *Herald*, 9 November 1860; George Edmonds, *Facts and Falsehoods Concerning the War on the South 1861-65* (Memphis, Tennessee: A.R. Taylor and Company, 1904), page 180. "George Edmonds" was the pseudonym of Elizabeth Meriwether of Memphis, Tennessee.

4. New York *Herald*, 11 November 1860; Edmonds, *ibid.*, page 176.

Horace Greeley

ertheless; and we do not see how one party can have a right to do what another party has a right to prevent. We must ever resist the asserted right of any State to remain in the Union and nullify or defy the laws thereof: to withdraw from the Union is quite another matter. And, whenever a considerable section of our Union shall deliberately resolve to go out, we shall resist all coercive measures designed to keep her in. We hope never to live in a republic whereof one section is pinned to the residue by bayonets.[5]

On the seventeenth of December, only three days before the secession of South Carolina, Greeley continued, "If it [the Declaration of Independence] justified the secession from the British Empire of three millions of colonists in 1776, we do not see why it would not justify the secession of five millions of Southrons from the Federal Union in 1861. If we are mistaken on this point, why does not some one attempt to show wherein and why?"[6] Of course, none of Greeley's fellow Republicans dared take up his challenge until after war hysteria had seized the North four months later, because they knew that the historical and constitutional evidence would not have

5. New York *Tribune*, 9 November 1860; Horace Greeley, *The American Conflict* (Hartford, Connecticut: O.D. Chase, 1866), Volume I, page 359.

6. New York *Tribune*, 17 December 1860; George Ticknor Curtis, *Life of James Buchanan, Fifteenth President of the United States* (New York: D. Appleton and Company, 1883), Volume II, page 430.

led rational minds to any other conclusion. Wendell Phillips, for example, responded to news of the secession of the Gulf States with these words: "'The covenant with death' is annulled; 'the agreement with hell' is broken to pieces. The chain which has held the slave system since 1787 is parted. Thirty years ago, Southern leaders, sixteen years ago, Northern Abolitionists, announced their purpose to seek the dissolution of the American Union. Who dreamed that success would come so soon?"[7] Senator Charles Sumner of Massachusetts said, "Nothing can possibly be so horrible, so wicked or so foolish as a war on the South."[8] Senator Benjamin F. Wade of Ohio, who was even more vocal in declaring "the States in their sovereignty" to be "the judge in the last resort of the violation of the Constitution of the United States," asserted "the rights of the States to protect their own citizens" against efforts "to consolidate this government into a miserable despotism."[9] On 4 December 1856, he had this to say on the floor of the Senate:

> If they [the Southern people] do not feel interested in upholding this Union – if it really en-

7. Wendell Phillips, speech on 20 January, 1861; in Wendell Phillips, *Speeches, Lectures, and Letters* (Boston: Walker, Wise and Company, 1864), page 343.

8. *North American Review* (October, 1879), page 378.

9. Hunter McGuire and George L. Christian, *The Confederate Cause and Conduct in the War Between the States* (Richmond, Virginia: L.H. Jenkins, Inc., 1907), page 43.

trenches on their rights – if it endangers their institutions to such an extent that they cannot feel secure under it – if their interests are violently assailed by the means of this Union, I am not one of those who expect that they will long continue under it. I am not one of those who ask them to continue in such a Union. It would be doing violence to the platform of the party to which I belong. We have adopted the old Declaration of Independence as the basis of our political movements, which declares that any people, when their Government ceases to protect their rights, when it is so subverted from the true purposes of government as to oppress them, have the right to recur to fundamental principles, and if need be, to destroy the Government under which they live, and to erect upon its ruins another conducive to their welfare. I hold that they have this right. I will not blame any people for exercising it, whenever they think the contingency has come. I certainly shall be an advocate of that same doctrine whenever I find that the principles of this Government have become so oppressive to the section to which I belong, that a free people ought no longer to endure it.... I hope the Union will continue forever. I believe it may continue forever. I see nothing at present which I think should dissolve it; but if other gentlemen see it, I say again that they have the same interest in maintaining this Union, in my judgment, as we of the North have. If they think they have not, be it so. You cannot forcibly hold men in the Union; for the attempt to do so, it seems to me, would subvert the first principles of the Government under which we live.[10]

On the eighteenth of December, 1860, Wade again stated, "I do not... so much blame the people of the South; because they believe, and they are led to believe by all the information that comes before them, that we, the dominant party to-day, who have just seized upon the reins of this Government, are their mortal enemies, and stand ready to trample their institutions under foot."[11] Wade's feigned sympathy was hardly convincing, for it had been the prominent members of the "dominant party" themselves, repeatedly in their own speeches and published works, who had led the Southern people to view them as "mortal enemies." The Senator's hypocrisy was further demonstrated when he made the following statements after the war had commenced:

> And, after all this, to talk of a Union! Sir, I have said you have no Union. I say you have no Union to-day worthy of the name. I am here a conservative man, knowing, as I do, that the only salvation to your Union is that you divest it entirely from all the taints of slavery. If we can't have that, then I go for no Union at all; but I go for a – fight![12]

---

10. Wade, speech delivered in the Senate on 4 December 1856; *Congressional Globe* (Thirty-Four Congress, Third Session), page 25.

11. *Ibid.* (Thirty-Sixth Congress, Second Session), page 100.

12. George Lunt, *The Origin of the Late War* (New York: D. Appleton and Company, 1866), page 388.

I would reduce the aristocratic slaveholders to utter poverty. I know they are conceited; I know they are essentially aristocratic. I am fully persuaded that their minds and their feelings are so in antagonism to Republican Democratic doctrines that it is impossible to reconcile them, and we shall never have peace until we have reduced the leaders to utter poverty, and taken thereby their influence away. I am for doing it. It ought to be done.[13]

In light of these facts, we must ask the question, Did the States of the North possess the right "to protect their own citizens" from "the violation of the Constitution of the United States" – or worse, from the threatened wholesale murder of helpless women and children threatened by many of the leading Abolitionists[14] – while the States of the South were

---

13. Speech on 25 June 1862; *Congressional Globe* (Thirty-Seventh Congress, Second Session); Stephen D. Carpenter, *The Logic of History: Five Hundred Political Texts Being Concentrated Extracts of Abolitionism* (Madison, Wisconson: Self-published, 1864), page 91.

14. The infamous anti-South assassin John Brown mentioned at the beginning of this book received financial support from six Republican leaders: Thomas Wentworth Higginson, Samuel Gridley Howe, Theodore Parker, Franklin Benjamin Sanborn, Gerrit Smith, and George Luther Steams. In the words of Parker, "A man held against his will, as a slave, has a natural right to kill any one who seeks to prevent his enjoyment of liberty. It may be a natural duty of a slave to develop this natural right in a practical manner, and actually kill those who seek to prevent his enjoyment of liberty.... It may be a natural charity for the freeman to help the slaves to the enjoyment of their lib-

somehow destitute of this right? Apparently so, for it should be noted that Greeley, Phillips, Sumner, and Wade would, only a few months later, become the most vicious mouthpieces of Republican hatred of the Southern people, calling for, at least in Wade's case, their utter destruction as a just punishment for merely asserting and acting upon the very ideals expressed by the Chicago Convention which nominated Abraham Lincoln in 1860:

> *Resolved*, That the maintenance inviolate of the rights of the States, and especially the right of each State to order and control its own domestic institutions, according to its own judgment exclusively, is essential to that balance of power on which the perfection and endurance of our political fabric depends, and we denounce the lawless invasion by armed force of the soil of any State or Territory, no matter what pretext, as among the gravest of crimes.[15]

---

erty, and as a means to that end, to aid them in killing all such as oppose their natural freedom" (Carpenter, *Logic of History*, page 67). These sentiments were not held merely by a few fanatics. The book entitled, *The Impending Crisis: How to Meet It*, authored by Hinton Rowan Helper, which was endorsed by every Republican in the United States Congress, including the future Secretary of State, William Seward, warned of "barbarous massacre by the negroes at night" and "a fate too horrible to contemplate" which would furnish "a more direful scene of atrocity and carnage" than the St. Bartholomew massacre [New York: A.B. Burdick, Publishers, 1857], page 147).

14. Thomas Hudson McKee, *National Conventions and Platforms of All Political Parties 1789-1900* (Baltimore, Mary-

On his way to Washington, D.C. to be inaugurated as the sixteenth President of the United States, Lincoln further elaborated on his party's platform in a speech which he delivered at his home in Springfield, Illinois: "What is 'invasion'? Would the marching of an army into South Carolina, without the consent of her people, and with hostile intent toward them be 'invasion'? I certainly think it would, and it would be 'coercion' also if South Carolinians were forced to submit."[16] Lincoln issued a call on 15 April 1861 for 75,000 troops to do this very thing, and thus was a criminal by his party's and his own definition of the word.

---

land: Friedenwald Company, 1900), page 68.

15. Lincoln, address to the Indiana State Legislature on 12 February 1861; *Harper's Weekly*, 23 February 1861, page 119; Horace Greeley, *American Conflict* (Hartford, Connecticut: O.D. Chase, 1866), Volume I, page 419.

King George III

APPENDIX ONE
The Nationalist Myth and the Fourth of July

Millions of Americans will soon gather in stadiums, parks, and other public venues across the country to celebrate a myth – one that has been carefully constructed over many years to elicit the highest levels of emotion and devotion, while just as carefully concealing the historical facts which undermine it. The myth: we commemorate the birth of our nation on the Fourth of July.

The truth is that there was no birth of an American nation on 4 July 1776. Instead, there was merely a joint declaration of independence of thirteen States from their former allegiance to the British Crown – an allegiance that each, while in their colonial condition, owed separately, not collectively, to the King via their individual charters. The official title of this declaration was "The unanimous Declaration of the thirteen united States of America." This was a shortened form of "The unanimous Declaration of Georgia, New York, Virginia, Massachusetts, *etc.*" According to the rules of English grammar, the lower case of the initial letter in the word "united" rendered it an adjective rather than a part of the proper noun which followed, thus identifying their association with each other as one of purpose, not of a political nature. Prior to 1781, the closest the several States had ever come to establishing a common political bond between themselves was the First Continental Congress, which met briefly in Philadelphia in 1774 and consisted of delegates from twelve of the colonies (Georgia was not represented), chosen to consider an economic boycott of British trade and to petition King George III for a redress of their grievances. The Second Continental Congress was simply a reconvening of the First, for the purpose of organizing a common defense of the colonies against British invasion and whose power was limited to issuing resolutions which had no legally binding authority whatsoever over the thirteen, either separately or jointly. In fact, the resolutions of the Congress and its requests for funding for the Continental Army were frequently ignored.

Another misconception that requires correction is that the independence of the States from Great Britain is legally dated from the signing of the Declaration on 4 July 1776. However, this is an inaccurate understanding of the purpose of that document, which was merely to serve as a notice and justification to the world of what had *already* transpired. For example, Virginia had declared its independence and adopted a State constitution on 29 June 1776, five days before the Declaration was signed. The people of each colony, separately and for themselves alone, determined that "as Free and Independent States," they should have "full Power to levy War, conclude Peace, contract Alliances, establish Commerce, and to do all other Acts and Things which Independent States may of right do." In other words, sovereignty had passed from the King to each new State separately, and not to the thirteen States as a collective body. Consequently the allegiance of each individual man, woman, and child was now owed to their own State as its Citizens rather than to the King as his subjects. This is how patriotism was understood at that time.

The thirteen States were again separately recognized as sovereign in the Articles of Confederation of 1781, in the Treaty of Paris of 1783, and again in the Constitution of 1787, particularly in the Tenth Amendment. Calling to mind the former title of the Declaration of Independence, the original wording of the Preamble to the Constitution read, "We, the people of the States of New Hampshire, Massachusetts, Rhode Island and Providence Plantations, Connecticut, New York, New Jersey, Pennsylvania, Delaware, Maryland, Virginia, North Carolina, South Carolina and Georgia do ordain and establish this Constitution...." This wording was later shortened to read, "We the People of the United States," but the meaning remained the same: the Constitution was being "ordained and established" by distinct States, each acting for itself in its own sovereign capacity.

This fact is clearly seen in Article VII, which states, "The ratification of the conventions of nine States, shall be sufficient for the establishment of this Constitution between the States so ratifying the same." In other words, the constitutional bond would exist only between those States ratifying it, therefore excluding the non-ratifying States from the political compact known as "The United States of America." As it turned out, two of the thirteen States – North Carolina and Rhode Island – did remain outside of the Union for many months and were treated by the newly-established Federal Government as foreign nations during that time.

It is noteworthy that the terms "nation" and "national" do not appear in the Constitution, except when referring to foreign nations. In fact, the term "federal" was deliberately chosen by the framers over "national" to describe the government created by the Constitution, thereby defining it as the offspring of the Union and the common agent of the ordaining sovereignties. The compacting States agreed to surrender certain enumerated powers to this common agent for the general welfare of all, while reserving to themselves the continued exercise of all other powers not so enumerated. One of the reserved rights of any sovereign when entering into political compact with other sovereignties is that of withdrawal should the arrangement fail to answer to its purpose. We find this reserved right expressly stated in the ratifications of three of the original thirteen States – Virginia, New York, and Rhode Island

– and accepted without question or objection from the other ten States. Declarations of sovereignty were also embodied in many of the State constitutions, such as that of Massachusetts, and the reserved right of secession was proclaimed numerous times throughout the first several decades following the ratification of the Constitution by both Northern and Southern States. Thus, it is beyond dispute that the United States of America were legally a confederacy, not a nation, and were repeatedly described as such in the writings of the earliest political commentators.

The theory of a unitarian American nation was not popularized until Joseph Story, of Massachusetts, published his *Commentaries on the Constitution* in 1833. In this extensive work, Story argued that the "people of the United States" in the preamble of the Constitution referred to the "people in the aggregate," rather than the people constituting several States, and that the States were therefore dependent upon the Union for their existence. Daniel Webster, also of Massachusetts, relied on this fallacy in his congressional debate with South Carolinian Senator John C. Calhoun that same year. Calhoun so soundly refuted this theory that it nearly completely vanished from the political scene, only to be resurrected thirty years later by Abraham Lincoln in his first inaugural address on 4 March 1861, and again in his address to Congress on 4 July 1861. In the latter speech, Lincoln declared the absurdity that "the Union created the States," rather than vice versa, and that therefore, secession by any State or

States was tantamount to treason. He further ex-
pounded this theme in his celebrated Gettysburg address on 19 November 1863, wherein he dated the
now-familiar idea of the "nation's birth" in 1776 and
claimed that Northern soldiers had shed, and were
shedding, their blood so that this imagined entity
"would not perish from the earth." Finally, during
the Reconstruction period, the Republican radicals in
Congress admitted that the war had been fought
against the Southern States to overthrow "the perni-
cious heresy of State sovereignty," and to consolidate forever the American people into a single nation
under an all-powerful central Government.

Unreconstructed Southerners refused to ob-
serve the Fourth of July for several decades after the
War Between the States because they saw it as a day
of mourning rather than one of celebration. Not only
had Lincoln chosen that day to deliver a virtual declaration of war against the founding principles of
American constitutionalism, but it was also the anni-
versary of the fall of Vicksburg in the West (by
which Lincoln's Government gained control of the
Mississippi River, effectively cutting the Southern
Confederacy in half) and of the defeat of Robert E.
Lee's army at Gettysburg in the East (which marked
the point of decline for Confederate military
strength). Moreover, they saw the terrible irony of
celebrating the independence of the original thirteen
States from an oppressive central government in
1776 when their own States had been so unjustly
denied their own independence and their people sub-

jugated to an even greater tyranny than that from which their forefathers had fought to free themselves. That there is an American nation today is obvious; in fact, it can more accurately be described as an empire. Not only does the central Government in Washington, D. C. claim ultimate sovereignty over the American people, but it also asserts the prerogative of controlling every aspect of their lives. In addition, it seeks to militarily impose its own ideas of democracy and freedom on other nations and people around the globe. However, the question remains: just when was this modern nation born, if not in 1776? One noted historian gave the answer:

> [After the war] the old decentralized federal republic became a new national polity that taxed the people directly, created an internal revenue bureau to collect these taxes, expanded the jurisdiction of federal courts, established a national currency and a national banking structure. The United States went to war in 1861 to preserve the Union; it emerged from war in 1865 having created a nation. Before 1861 the two words "United States" were generally used as a plural noun: "The United States are a republic." After 1865 the United States became a singular noun. The loose union of states became a nation.[1]

Tyrants throughout history have understood

---

1. James M. McPherson, *Abraham Lincoln and the Second American Revolution* (New York: Oxford University Press, 1990), page viii.

that in order to keep a subjugated people under control, they must be cut off from their own history and provided with an alternate view of reality that is constantly reinforced through its symbols, ceremonies, and fabricated traditions. "[The conquered] must at least retain the semblance of the old forms," wrote Niccolo Machiavelli, the renowned political philosopher of the early Sixteenth Century, "so that it may seem to the people that there has been no change in the institutions, even though in fact they are entirely different from the old ones. For the great majority of mankind are satisfied with appearances, as though they were realities, and are often even more influenced by the things that seem than by those that are." Such is the power of this myth-making that the people will not only automatically react negatively against dissent from the accepted view, but they will also be willing to die, or to kill, for it. The ancient Grecian and Roman empires, and the more recent Nazi and Soviet regimes of the Twentieth Century, all relied on the power of propaganda and pageantry to control the public and are standing testimonies to the truth of Ecclesiastes 1:9: "The thing that hath been, it is that which shall be; and that which is done is that which shall be done: and there is no new thing under the sun."

APPENDIX TWO
John C. Calhoun's Response
to Daniel Webster
Congressional Globe – 26 February 1833

The Senator from Massachusetts in his argument against the Resolutions, directed his attack almost exclusively against the first; on the ground, I suppose, that it was the basis of the other two, and that, unless the first could be demolished, the others would follow of course. In this he was right. As plain and as simple as the facts contained in the first are, they cannot be admitted to be true without admitting the doctrines for which I, and the State I represent, contend. He commenced his attack with a verbal criticism on the Resolution, in the course of which he objected strongly to two words, "constitutional" and "accede." To the former, on the ground that the word, as used (constitutional compact), was obscure – that it conveyed no definite meaning – and that Constitution was a noun-substantive, and not an adjective. I regret that I have exposed myself to the criticism of the Senator. I certainly did not intend to use any expression of doubtful sense, and if I have done so, the Senator must attribute it to the poverty of my language, and not to design. I trust, however, that the Senator will excuse me, when he comes to hear my apology. In matters of criticism, authority is of the highest importance, and I have an authority of so high a character, in this case, for using the expression which he considers so obscure and so unconstitutional, as will justify me even in his eyes. It is no less than the authority of the Senator himself – given on a solemn occasion (the discussion on Mr. Foote's Resolution), and doubtless with great deliberation, after having duly weighed the force of the expression:

> Nevertheless, I do not complain, nor would I countenance any movement to alter this arrangement of representation. It is the original bargain – the Compact – let it stand – let the advantage of it be fully enjoyed. The Union itself is too full of benefits to be hazarded in propositions for changing its original basis. I go for the Constitution, as it is, and for the Union, as it is. But I am resolved not to submit, in silence, to accusations, either against myself, individually, or against the North, wholly unfounded and unjust – accusations which impute to us a disposition to evade the *Constitutional compact*, and to extend the power of the Government over the internal laws and domestic condition of the States.

It will be seen by this extract that the Senator

not only used the phrase "constitutional compact," which he now so much condemns, but, what is still more important, he calls the Constitution a compact – a bargain – which contains important admissions, having a direct and powerful bearing on the main issue, involved in the discussion, as will appear in the sequel. But, strong as his objection is to the word "constitutional," it is still stronger to the word "accede," which, he thinks, has been introduced into the Resolution with some deep design, as I suppose, to entrap the Senate into an admission of the doctrine of State Rights. Here, again, I must shelter myself under authority. But I suspect the Senator, by a sort of instinct (for our instincts often strangely run before our knowledge), had a prescience, which would account for his aversion for the word, that this authority was no less than Thomas Jefferson himself, the great apostle of the doctrine of State Rights. The word was borrowed from him. It was taken from the Kentucky Resolutions, as well as the substance of the resolution itself. But I trust I may neutralize whatever aversion the authorship of this word may have excited in the mind of the Senator, by the introduction of another authority – that of Washington, himself – who, in his speech to Congress, speaking of the admission of North Carolina into the Union, uses this very term, which was repeated by the Senate in their reply. Yet, in order to narrow the ground between the Senator and myself as much as possible, I will accommodate myself to his strange antipathy against the two unfortunate words, by striking them

out of the Resolution, and substituting in their place
those very words which the Senator himself has des-
ignated as constitutional phrases. In the place of that
abhorred adjective "constitutional," I will insert the
very noun substantive "constitution;" and, in the
place of the word "accede," I will insert the word
"ratify," which he designates as the proper term to
be used.

As proposed to be amended, the Resolution
would read:

> Resolved, That the people of the several
> States composing these United States are united as
> parties to a compact, under the title of the Consti-
> tution of the United States, which the people of
> each State ratified as a separate and Sovereign
> community, each binding itself by its own particular
> ratification; and that the Union of which the said
> compact is the bond, is a union *between* the States
> ratifying the same.

Where, sir, I ask, is that plain case of revolution? Where that hiatus, as wide as the globe, between the premises and the conclusion, which the
Senator proclaimed would be apparent, if the
Resolution was reduced into constitutional language? For my part, with my poor powers of conception, I cannot perceive the slightest difference between the Resolution, as first introduced, and as it is
proposed to be amended in conformity to the views
of the Senator. And, instead of that hiatus between
the premises and conclusion, which seems to startle
the imagination of the Senator, I can perceive noth-

ing but a continuous and solid surface, sufficient to sustain the magnificent superstructure of State Rights. Indeed, it seems to me that the Senator's vision is distorted by the medium through which he views every thing connected with the subject; and that the same distortion which has presented to his imagination this hiatus, as wide as the globe, where not even a fissure exists, also presented that beautiful and classical image of a strong man struggling in a bog, without the power of extricating himself, and incapable of being aided by any friendly hand; while, instead of struggling in a bog, he stands on the everlasting rock of truth.

Having now noticed the criticisms of the Senator, I shall proceed to meet and repel the main assault on the Resolution. He directed his attack against the strong point, the very horn of the citadel of State Rights. The Senator clearly perceived that, if the Constitution be a compact, it was impossible to deny the assertions contained in the Resolutions, or to resist the consequences which I had drawn from them, and, accordingly, directed his whole fire against that point; but, after so vast an expenditure of ammunition, not the slightest impression, so far as I can perceive, has been made. But to drop the simile, after a careful examination of the notes which I took of what the Senator said, I am now at a loss to know whether, in the opinion of the Senator, our Constitution is a compact or not, though the almost entire argument of the Senator was directed to that point. At one time he would seem to deny directly and positively that it was a compact, while at another he would appear, in language not less strong, to admit that it was.

I have collated all that the Senator has said upon this point; and, that what I have stated may not appear exaggerated, I will read his remarks in juxtaposition. He said that, "The Constitution means a Government, not a compact." "Not a constitutional compact, but a Government." "If compact, it rests on plighted faith, and the mode of redress would be to declare the whole void." "States may secede, if a league or compact."

I thank the Senator for these admissions, which I intend to use hereafter.

"The States agreed that each should participate in the sovereignty of the other." Certainly, a very correct conception of the Constitution; but where did they make that agreement but by the Constitution, and how could they agree but by compact?

"The system, not a compact between States in their sovereign capacity, but a Government proper, founded on the adoption of the people, and creating individual relations between itself and the citizens." This, the Senator lays down as a leading, fundamental principle to sustain his doctrine, and, I must say, with strange confusion and uncertainty of language; not, certainly, to be explained by any want of command of the most appropriate words on his part.

"It does not call itself a compact, but a constitution. The Constitution rests on compact, but it is no longer a compact." I would ask, to what compact does the Senator refer, as that on which the Constitution rests? Before the adoption of the present Constitution, the States had formed but one compact, and that was the old Confederation; and, certainly, the gentleman does not intend to assert that the present Constitution rests upon that. What, then, is his meaning? What can it be, but that the Constitution itself is a compact? And how will his language read, when fairly interpreted, but that the Constitution was a compact, but is no longer a compact? It had, by some means or another, changed its nature, or become defunct.

He next states that "A man is almost untrue to his country who calls the Constitution a compact." I fear the Senator, in calling it a compact, a bargain, has called down this heavy denunciation on his own head. He finally states that "It is founded on compact, but not a compact." "It is the result of a compact." To what are we to attribute this strange confusion of words? The Senator has a mind of high order, and perfectly trained to the most exact use of language. No man knows better the precise import of the words he uses. The difficulty is not in him, but in his subject. He who undertakes to prove that this Constitution is not a compact, undertakes a task which, be his strength ever so great, must oppress him by its weight. Taking the whole of the argument of the Senator together, I would say that it is his impression that the Constitution is not a compact, and will now proceed to consider the reason which he has assigned for this opinion.

He thinks there is an incompatibility between *constitution* and *compact*. To prove this, he adduces the words "ordain and establish," contained in the preamble of the Constitution. I confess I am not capable of perceiving in what manner these words are incompatible with the idea that the Constitution is a compact. The Senator will admit that a single State may ordain a constitution; and where is the difficulty, where the incompatibility, of two States concurring in ordaining and establishing a constitution? As between the States themselves, the instrument would be a compact; but in reference to the Government, and those on whom it operates, it would be ordained and established – ordained and established by the joint authority of two, instead of the single authority of one.

The next argument which the Senator advances to show that the language of the Constitution is irreconcilable with the idea of its being a compact, is taken from that portion of the instrument which imposes prohibitions on the authority of the States. He said that the language used, in imposing the prohibitions, is the language of a superior to an inferior; and that, therefore, it was not the language of a compact, which implies the equality of the parties. As a proof, the Senator cited several clauses of the Constitution which provide that no State shall enter into treaties of alliance and confederation, lay imposts, *etc.*, without the assent of Congress. If he had turned to the Articles of the old Confederation, which he acknowledges to have been a compact, he would have found that those very prohibitory articles of the Constitution were borrowed from that instrument; that the language, which he now considers as implying superiority, was taken *verbatim* from it. If he had extended his researches still further, he would have found that it is the habitual language used in treaties, whenever a stipulation is made against the performance of any act. Among many instances, which I could cite, if it were necessary, I refer the Senator to the celebrated treaty negotiated by Mr. Jay with Great Britain, in 1793, in which the very language used in the Constitution is employed.

To prove that the Constitution is not a compact, the Senator next observes that it stipulates nothing, and asks, with an air of triumph, "Where are the evidences of the stipulations between the States?" I must express my surprise at this interrogatory, coming from so intelligent a source. Has the Senator never seen the ratifications of the Constitution by the several States? Did he not cite them on this very occasion? Do they contain no evidence of stipulations on the part of the States? Nor is the assertion less strange that the Constitution contains no stipulations. So far from regarding it in the light in which the Senator regards it, I consider the whole instrument but a mass of stipulations. What is that but a stipulation to which the Senator refers when he states, in the course of his argument, that each State had agreed to participate in the sovereignty of the others.

But the principal argument on which the Senator relied to show that the Constitution is not a compact, rests on the provision, in that instrument, which declares that "this Constitution, and laws made in pursuance thereof, and treaties made under their authority, are the supreme law of the land." He asked, with marked emphasis, "Can a compact be the supreme law of the land?" His argument, in fact, as conclusively proves that treaties are not compacts as that the Constitution is not a compact. I might rest the issue on this decisive answer; but, as I desire to leave not a shadow of doubt on this important point, I shall follow the gentleman in the course of his reasoning.

He defines a Constitution to be a fundamental law, which organizes the Government, and points out the mode of its action. I will not object to the definition, though, in my opinion, a more appropriate one, or, at least, one better adapted to American ideas, could be given. My objection is not to the definition, but to the attempt to prove that the fundamental laws of a State cannot be a compact, as the Senator seems to suppose. I hold the very reverse to be the case; and that, according to the most approved writers on the subject of Government, these very fundamental laws which are now stated not only not to be compacts, but inconsistent with the very idea of compacts, are held invariably to be compacts; and, in that character, are distinguished from the ordinary laws of the country. I will cite a single authority, which is full and explicit on this point, from a writer of the highest repute.

Burlamaqui says, vol. ii, part 1, chap. i, secs. 35, 36, 37, 38:

It entirely depends upon a free people to invest the Sovereigns, whom they place over their heads, with an authority either absolute or limited by certain laws. These regulations, by which the supreme authority is kept within bounds, are called *the fundamental laws of the State*. The fundamental laws of a State, taken in their full extent, are not only the decrees by which the entire body of the nation determine the form of Government, and the manner of succeeding to the Crown, but are likewise covenants between the people and the person on whom they confer the Sovereignty, which regulate the manner of governing, and by which the supreme authority is limited.

These regulations are called fundamental laws, because they are the basis, as it were, and foundation of the State on which the structure of the Government is raised, and, because the people look upon these regulations as their principal strength and support.

The name of laws, however, has been given to these regulations in an improper and figurative sense, for, properly speaking, they are real covenants. But as these covenants are obligatory between the contracting parties, they have the force of laws themselves.

The same, vol. ii, part 2, ch. i, secs. 19 and 22, in part:

The whole body of the nation, in whom the

supreme power originally resides, may regulate the Government by a fundamental law, in such manner, as to commit the exercise of the different parts of the supreme power to different persons or bodies, who may act independently of each other in regard to the rights committed to them, but still subordinate to the laws from which those rights are derived.

And these fundamental laws are real covenants, or what the civilians call *pacta conventa*, between the different orders of the republic, by which they stipulate that each shall have a particular part of the Sovereignty, and that this shall establish the form of Government. It is evident that, by these means, each of the contracting parties acquires a right, not only of exercising the power granted to it, but also of preserving that original right.

A reference to the constitution of Great Britain, with which we are better acquainted than with that of any other European Government, will show that that is a compact. Magna Charta may certainly be reckoned among the fundamental laws of that kingdom. Now, although it did not assume, originally, the form of a compact, yet, before the breaking up of the meeting of the Barons which imposed it on King John, it was reduced into the form of a covenant, and duly signed by Robert Fitzwalter and others, on the one part, and the King on the other.

But we have a more decisive proof that the Constitution of England is a compact, in the resolution of the Lords and Commons, in 1688, which declared, "King James the Second, having endeavored to subvert the constitution of the kingdom, by breaking the original contract between the King and people, and having, by the advice of Jesuits and other wicked persons, violated the fundamental law, and withdrawn himself out of the kingdom, hath abdicated the Government, and that the throne is thereby become vacant."

But why should I refer to writers upon the subject of Government, or inquire into the constitution of foreign States, when there are such decisive proofs that our Constitution is a compact? On this point the Senator is estopped. I borrow from the gentleman, and thank him for the word. His adopted State, which he so ably represents on this floor, and his native State, the States of Massachusetts and New Hampshire, both declared, in their ratification of the Constitution, that it was a compact. The ratification of Massachusetts is in the following words:

> The Convention having impartially discussed, and fully considered, the Constitution for the United States of America, reported to Congress by the Convention of Delegates from the United States of America, and submitted to us by a resolution of the General Court of the said commonwealth, passed the 25th day of October last past, and acknowledging, with grateful hearts, the goodness of the Supreme Ruler of the universe in affording the people of the United States, in the course of his providence, an opportunity, deliberately and peaceably, without fraud or surprise, of entering in-

to an explicit and solemn compact with each other, by assenting to and ratifying a new Constitution, in order to form a more perfect union, establish justice, insure domestic tranquillity, provide for the common defence, promote the general welfare, and secure the blessings of liberty to themselves and their posterity, do, in the name and in behalf of the people of the commonwealth of Massachusetts, assent to and ratify the said Constitution for the United States of America.

The ratification of New Hampshire is taken from that of Massachusetts, and almost in the same words. But proof, if possible, still more decisive, may be found in the celebrated resolutions of Virginia on the alien and sedition law, in 1798, and the responses of Massachusetts and the other States. These resolutions expressly assert that the Constitution is a compact between the States, in the following language:

That this Assembly doth explicitly and peremptorily declare, that it views the powers of the federal government, as resulting from the compact, to which the States are parties; as limited by the plain sense and intention of the instrument constituting the compact; as no further valid than they are authorized by the grants enumerated in that compact; and that in case of a deliberate, palpable, and dangerous exercise of other powers, not granted by the said compact, the States who are parties thereto, have the right, and are in duty bound, to interpose for arresting the progress of the evil, and for

John C. Calhoun

maintaining within their respective limits, the authorities, rights and liberties appertaining to them.

That the General Assembly doth also express its deep regret, that a spirit has in sundry instances, been manifested by the federal government, to enlarge its powers by forced constructions of the constitutional charter which defines them; and that implications have appeared of a design to expound certain general phrases (which having been copied from the very limited grant of power in the former Articles of Confederation were the less liable to be misconstrued) so as to destroy the meaning and effect of the particular enumeration which necessarily explains and limits the general phrases; and so as to consolidate the States by degrees, into one sovereignty, the obvious tendency and inevitable consequence of which would be, to transform the present republican system of the United States into an absolute, or at best a mixed monarchy.

They were sent to the several States. We have the replies of Delaware, New York, Connecticut, New Hampshire, Vermont, and Massachusetts, not one of which contradicts this important assertion on the part of Virginia; and, by their silence, they all acquiesce in its truth.

Now, I ask the Senator himself – I put it to his candor to say, if South Carolina be estopped on the subject of the protective system, because Mr. Burke and Mr. Smith proposed a moderate duty on hemp, or some other article, I know not what, nor do I care, with a view of encouraging its production (of which motion, I venture to say, not one individual in a hundred in the State ever heard), whether he and Massachusetts, after this clear, full, and solemn recognition that the Constitution is a compact (both on his part and that of his State), be not forever estopped on this important point?

There remains one more of the Senator's arguments, to prove that the Constitution is not a compact, to be considered. He says it is not a compact, because it is a Government; which he defines to be an organized body, possessed of the will and power to execute its purposes by its own proper authority; and which, he says, bears not the slightest resemblance to a compact. But I would ask the Senator, Whoever considered a Government, when spoken of as the agent to execute the powers of the Constitution, and distinct from the Constitution itself, as a compact? In that light it would be a perfect absurdity. It is true that, in general and loose language, it is often said that the Government is a compact, meaning the Constitution which created it, and vested it with authority to execute the powers contained in the instrument; but when the distinction is drawn between the Constitution and the Government, as the Senator has done, it would be as ridiculous to call the Government a compact, as to call an individual, appointed to execute the provisions of a contract, a contract; and not less so to suppose that there could be the slightest resemblance between them. In connection with this point, the Senator, to prove that the Constitution is not a compact, asserts that it is wholly independent of the State and pointedly declares that the States have not a right to touch a hair of its head; and this, with that provision in the Constitution that three-fourths of the States have a right to alter, change, amend, or even to abolish it, staring him in the face.

I have examined all of the arguments of the Senator intended to prove that the Constitution is not a compact; and I trust I have shown, by the clearest demonstration, that his arguments are perfectly inconclusive, and that his assertion is against the clearest and most solemn evidence – evidence of record, and of such a character that it ought to close his lips forever.

I turn now to consider the other, and, apparently contradictory aspect in which the Senator presented this part of the subject: I mean that in which he states that the Government is founded in compact, but is no longer a compact. I have already remarked, that no other interpretation could be given to this assertion, except that the Constitution was once a compact, but is no longer so. There was a vagueness and indistinctness in this part of the Senator's argument, which left me altogether uncertain as to its real meaning. If he meant, as I presume he did, that the compact is an executed, and not an executory one – that its object was to create a Government, and to invest it with proper authority – and that, having executed this office, it had performed its functions, and, with it, had ceased to exist, then we have the extraordinary avowal that, the Constitution is a dead letter – that it had ceased to have any binding effect, or any practical influence or operation.

It has, indeed, often been charged that the Constitution has become a dead letter; that it is continually violated, and has lost all its control over the Government; but no one has ever before been bold enough to advance a theory on the avowed basis that it was an executed, and, therefore, an extinct instrument. I will not seriously attempt to refute an argument, which, to me, appears so extravagant. I had thought that the Constitution was to endure forever; and that, so far from its being an executed contract, it contained great trust powers for the benefit of those who created it, and of all future generations – which never could be finally executed during the existence of the world, if our Government should so long endure.

I will now return to the first Resolution, to see how the issue stands between the Senator from Massachusetts and myself. It contains three propositions. First, that the Constitution is a compact; second, that it was formed by the States, constituting distinct communities; and, lastly, that it is a subsisting and binding compact between the States. How do these three propositions now stand? The first, I trust, has been satisfactorily established; the second, the Senator has admitted, faintly, indeed, but still he has admitted it to be true. This admission is something. It is so much gained by discussion. Three years ago even this was a contested point. But I cannot say that I thank him for the admission; we owe it to the force of truth. The fact that these States were declared to be free and independent States at the time of their independence; that they were acknowledged to be so by Great Britain in the treaty which terminated the war of the Revolution, and secured their independence; that they were recognized in the same character in the old Articles of the Confederation; and, finally, that the present Constitution was formed by a Convention of the several States; afterwards submitted to them for their respective ratifications, and was ratified by them separately, each for itself, and each, by its own act, binding its citizens – formed a body of facts too clear to be denied, and too strong to be resisted.

It now remains to consider the third and last proposition contained in the Resolution, – that it is a binding and a subsisting compact between the States. The Senator was not explicit on this point. I understood him, however, as asserting that, though formed by the States, the Constitution was not binding between the States as distinct communities, but between the American people in the aggregate; who, in consequence of the adoption of the Constitution, according to the opinion of the Senator, became one people, at least to the extent of the delegated powers. This would, indeed, be a great change. All acknowledge that, previous to the adoption of the Constitution, the States constituted distinct and independent communities, in full possession of their Sovereignty; and, surely, if the adoption of the Constitution was intended to effect the great and important change in their condition which the theory of the Senator supposes, some evidence of it ought to be found in the instrument itself. It professes to be a careful and full enumeration of all the powers which the States delegated, and of every modification of their political condition. The Senator said that he looked to the Constitution in order to ascertain its real character; and, surely, he ought to look to the same instrument in order to ascertain what changes were, in fact, made in the political condition of the States and the country. But, with the exception of "we, the people of the United States," in the preamble, he has not pointed out a single indication in the Constitution, of the great change which as he conceives, has been effected in this respect.

Now, sir, I intend to prove, that the only argument on which the gentleman relies on this point, must utterly fail him. I do not intend to go into a critical examination of the expression of the preamble to which I have referred. I do not deem it necessary. But if it were, it might be easily shown that it is at least as applicable to my view of the Constitution as to that of the Senator; and that the whole of his argument on this point rests on the ambiguity of the term *thirteen United States*; which may mean certain territorial limits, comprehending within them the whole of the States and Territories of the Union. In this sense, the people of the United States may mean *all* the people living within these limits, without reference to the States or Territories in which they may reside, or of which they may be citizens; and it is in this sense only, that the expression gives the least countenance to the argument of the Senator.

But it may also mean, *the States united*, which inversion alone, without further explanation, removes the ambiguity to which I have referred. The expression in this sense, obviously means no more than to speak of the people of the several States in their united and confederated capacity; and, if it were requisite, it might be shown that it is only in this sense that the expression is used in the Constitution. But it is not necessary. A single argument will forever settle this point. Whatever may be the true meaning of the expression, it is not applicable to the condition of the States as they exist under the Constitution, but as it was under the old Confederation, before its adoption. The Constitution had not yet been adopted, and the States, in ordaining it, could only speak of themselves in the condition in which they then existed, and not in that in which they would exist under the Constitution. So that, if the argument of the Senator proves any thing, it proves, not (as he supposes) that the Constitution forms the American people into an aggregate mass of individuals, but that such was their political condition before its adoption, under the old Confederation, directly contrary to his argument in the previous part of this discussion.

But I intend not to leave this important point, the last refuge of those who advocate consolidation, even on this conclusive argument. I have shown that the Constitution affords not the least evidence of the mighty change of the political condition of the States and the country, which the Senator supposed it effected; and I intend now, by the most decisive proof, drawn from the instrument itself, to show that no such change was intended, and that the people of the States are united under it as States, and not as individuals. On this point there is a very important part of the Constitution entirely and strangely overlooked by the Senator in this debate, as it is expressed in the first Resolution, which furnishes conclusive evidence not only that the Constitution is a compact, but a subsisting compact, binding between the States. I allude to the seventh Article, which provides that the ratification of the Conventions of nine States shall be sufficient for the establishment of this Constitution *"between the States* so ratifying the same."* Yes, *"between the States."* These little words mean a volume. Compacts, not laws, bind *between* States; and it here binds, not as between individuals, but between *the States*: the States *ratifying*; implying, as strong as language can make it, that the Constitution is what I have asserted it to be – a compact, ratified by the States, and a subsisting compact, binding the States ratifying it.

But, sir, I will not leave this point, all-important in establishing the true theory of our Government, on this argument alone, as demonstrative and conclusive as I hold it to be. Another, not much less powerful, but of a different character, may be drawn from the tenth amended Article, which provides that the powers not delegated to the United States by the

Constitution, nor prohibited by it to the States, are reserved to the States respectively or to the people. The Article of Ratification, which I have just cited, informs us that the Constitution, which delegates powers, was ratified by the States, and is binding between them. This informs us to whom the powers are delegated – a most important fact in determining the point immediately at issue between the Senator and myself. According to his views, the Constitution created a union between individuals, if the solecism may be allowed, and that it formed, at least to the extent of the powers delegated, one people, and not a Federal Union of the States, as I contend; or, to express the same idea differently, that the delegation of powers was to the American people in the aggregate (for it is only by such delegation that they could be constituted one people), and not to the *United States* – directly contrary to the Article just cited, which declares that the powers are delegated to the United States. And here it is worthy of notice, that the Senator cannot shelter himself under the ambiguous phrase, "to the people of the United States," under which he would certainly have taken refuge, had the Constitution so expressed it; but fortunately for the cause of truth and the great principles of constitutional liberty for which I am contending, "people" is omitted: thus making the delegation of power clear and unequivocal to the *United States*, as distinct political communities, and conclusively proving that all the powers delegated are reciprocally delegated by the States to each other, as distinct political communities.

So much for the delegated powers. Now, as all admit, and as it is expressly provided for in the Constitution, the *reserved* powers are reserved "to the States *respectively*, or to the people." None will pretend that, as far as they are concerned, we are one people, though the argument to prove it, however absurd, would be far more plausible than that which goes to show that we are one people to the extent of the delegated powers. This reservation "to the people" might, in the hands of subtle and trained logicians, be a peg to hang a doubt upon; and had the expression "to the people" been connected, as fortunately it is not, with the delegated instead of the reserved powers, we should not have heard of this in the present discussion.

I have now established, I hope, beyond the power of controversy, every allegation contained in the first Resolution – that the Constitution is a compact formed by the people of the several States, as distinct political communities, and subsisting and binding between the States in the same character; which brings me to the consideration of the consequences which may be fairly deduced, in reference to the character of our political system, from these established facts.

The first and most important is, they conclusively establish that ours is a Federal system – a system of States arranged in a Federal Union, each retaining its distinct existence and sovereignty. Ours has every attribute which belongs to a Federative System. It is founded on compact; it is formed by sovereign communities, and is binding between them in their sovereign capacity. I might appeal, in confirmation of this assertion, to all elementary writers on the subject of Government, but will content myself with citing one only. Burlamaqui, quoted with approbation by Judge Tucker, in his *Commentary on Blackstone*, himself a high authority, says:

> Political bodies, whether great or small, if they are constituted by a people formerly independent, and under no civil subjection, or by those who justly claim independence from any civil power they were formerly subject to, have the civil supremacy in themselves, and are in a state of equal right and liberty with respect to all other States, whether great or small. No regard is to be had in this matter to names, whether the body-politic be called a kingdom, an empire, a principality, a dukedom, a country, a republic, or free town. If it can exercise justly all the essential parts of civil power within itself, independently of any other person or body-politic – and no other has any right to rescind or annul its acts – it has the civil supremacy, how small soever its territory may be, or the number of its people, and has all the rights of an independent State.

> This independence of States, and their being distinct political bodies from each other, is not obstructed by any alliance or confederacies whatsoever, about exercising jointly any parts of the supreme powers, such as those of peace and war, in league offensive and defensive. Two States, notwithstanding such treaties, are separate bodies, and

independent.

These are, then, only deemed politically united, when some one person or council is constituted with a right to exercise some essential powers for both, and to hinder either from exercising them separately. If any person or council is empowered to exercise all these essential powers for both, they are then one State: such is the State of England and Scotland, since the Act of Union made at the beginning of the eighteenth century, whereby the two kingdoms were incorporated into one, all parts of the supreme power of both kingdoms being thenceforward united, and vested in the three Estates of the realm of Great Britain; by which entire coalition, though both kingdoms retain their ancient laws and usages in many respects, they are as effectually united and incorporated, as the several petty kingdoms, which composed the heptarchy, were before that period.

But when only a portion of the supreme civil power is vested in one person or council for both, such as that of peace and war, or of deciding controversies between different States, or their subjects, while each, within itself, exercises other parts of the supreme power, independently of all the others – in this case they are called *Systems of States*, which Burlamaqui defines to be an assemblage of perfect Governments, strictly united by some common bond, so that they seem to make but a single body with respect to those affairs which interest them in common, though each preserves its Sovereignty, full and entire, independently of all others. And in this case, he adds, the Confederate

States engage to each other only to exercise, with common consent, certain parts of the Sovereignty, especially that which relates to their mutual defence against foreign enemies. But each of the Confederates retains an entire liberty of exercising, as it thinks proper, those parts of the Sovereignty which are not mentioned in the treaty of Union, as parts that ought to be exercised in common. And of this nature is the American Confederacy, in which each State has resigned the exercise of certain parts of the supreme civil power which they possessed before (except in common with the other States included in the Confederacy), reserving to themselves all their former powers, which are not delegated to the United States by the common bond of Union.

A visible distinction, and not less important than obvious, occurs to our observation, in comparing these different kinds of Union. The kingdoms of England and Scotland are united into one kingdom; and the two contracting States, by such an incorporate Union, are, in the opinion of Judge Blackstone, totally annihilated, without any power of revival; and a third arises from their conjunction, in which all the rights of Sovereignty, and particularly that of Legislation, are vested. From whence he expresses a doubt, whether any infringements of the fundamental and essential conditions of the Union would, of itself, dissolve the Union of those kingdoms; though he readily admits that, in the case of a *Federate* alliance, such an infringement would certainly rescind the compact between the Confederated States. In the United States of America, on the contrary, each State retains its own antecedent form of Government; its own laws, subject to the alteration and control of its own Legislature only; its own executive officers and council of State; its own courts of Judicature, its own judges, its own magistrates, civil officers, and officers of the militia; and, in short, its own civil State, or body politic, in every respect whatsoever. And by the express declaration of the 10th article of the amendments to the Constitution, the powers not delegated to the United States by the Constitution, nor prohibited by it to the States, are reserved to the States respectively, or to the people. In Great Britain, a new *civil State* is created by the annihilation of two antecedent civil States; in the American States, a general *Federal* council and administration is provided, for the joint exercise of such of their several powers as can be more conveniently exercised in that mode than any other, leaving their *civil State* unaltered; and all the other powers, which the States antecedently possessed, to be exercised by them respectively, as if no Union or connection were established between them.

The ancient Achaia seems to have been a Confederacy founded upon a similar plan; each of those little States had its distinct possessions, territories, and boundaries; each had its Senate or Assembly, its magistrates and judges; and every State sent Deputies to the General Convention, and had equal weight in all determinations. And most of the neighboring States which, moved by fear of danger, acceded to this Confederacy, had reason to felicitate themselves.

These Confederacies, by which several States

are united together by a perpetual league of alliance, are chiefly founded upon this circumstance, that each particular people choose to remain their own masters, and yet are not strong enough to make head against a common enemy. The purport of such an agreement usually is, that they shall not exercise some part of the Sovereignty, there specified, without the general consent of each other. For the leagues, to which these systems of States owe their rise, seem distinguished from others (so frequent among different States), chiefly by this consideration, that, in the latter, each confederate people determine themselves, by their own judgment, to certain mutual performances; yet so that, in all other respects, they design not, in the least, to make the exercise of that part of the Sovereignty, whence these performances proceed, dependent on the consent of their allies, or to retrench any thing from their full and unlimited power of governing their own States. Thus, we see that ordinary treaties propose, for the most part, as their aim, only some particular advantage of the States thus transacting – their interests happening, at present, to fall in with each other – but do not produce any lasting union as to the chief management of affairs. Such was the treaty of alliance between America and France, in the year 1778, by which, among other articles, it was agreed that neither of the two parties should conclude either truce or peace with Great Britain, without the formal consent of the other, first obtained, and whereby they mutually engaged not to lay down their arms until the independence of the United States should be formally or tacitly assured by the treaty or treaties which should terminate the war. Whereas, in these confederacies of which we are now speaking, the contrary is observable, they being established with this design, that the several States shall forever link their safety, one with another; and, in order to their mutual defence, shall engage themselves not to exercise certain parts of their Sovereign power, otherwise than by a common agreement and approbation. Such were the stipulations, among others, contained in the Articles of Confederation and perpetual Union between American States, by which it was agreed that no State should, without the consent of the United States, in Congress assembled, send any embassy to, or receive any embassy from, or enter into any conference, agreement, alliance or treaty with, any king, prince or State; nor keep up any vessels of war, or body of forces, in time of peace; nor engage in any war, without the consent of the United States in Congress assembled, unless actually invaded; nor grant commissions to any ships of war, or letters of marque and reprisal, except after a declaration of war by the United States in Congress assembled, with several others; yet each State, respectively, retains its Sovereignty, freedom and independence, and every power, jurisdiction and right which is not expressly delegated to the United States in Congress assembled. The promises made in these two cases, here compared, run very differently; in the former, thus: I will join you, in this particular war, as a confederate, and the manner of our attacking the enemy shall be concerted by our common advice; nor will we desist

from war, till the particular end thereof, the establishment of the independence of the United States,
be obtained in the latter, thus: None of us who have
entered into this alliance, will make use of our right
as to the affairs of war and peace, except by the
general consent of the whole confederacy. We observed before that these Unions submit only some
certain parts of the Sovereignty to mutual direction;
for it seems hardly possible that the affairs of different States should have so close a connection, as
that all and each of them should look on it as their
interest to have no part of the chief Government
exercised without the general concurrence. The
most convenient method, therefore, seems to be,
that the particular States reserve to themselves all
those branches of the supreme authority, the management of which can have little or no influence in
the affairs of the rest.

If we compare our present system with the old
Confederation, which all acknowledge to have been
Federal in its character, we shall find that it pos-
sesses all the attributes which belong to that form of
Government as fully and completely as that did. In
fact, *in this particular*, there is but a single difference, and that not essential, as regards the point
immediately under consideration, though very important in other respects. The Confederation was the
act of the State Governments, and formed a union of
Governments. The present Constitution is the act of
the States themselves, or, which is the same thing, of
the people of the several States, and forms a union of
them as Sovereign communities. The States, previous

to the adoption of the Constitution, were as separate and distinct political bodies as the Governments which represent them, and there is nothing in the nature of things to prevent them from uniting under a compact, in a Federal Union, without being blended in one mass, any more than uniting the Governments themselves, in like manner, without merging them in a single Government. To illustrate what I have stated by reference to ordinary transactions, the Confederation was a contract between agents – the present Constitution a contract between the principals themselves; or, to take a more analogous case, one is a League made by ambassadors; the other, a League made by Sovereigns – the latter no more tending to unite the parties into a single Sovereignty than the former. The only difference is in the solemnity of the act and the force of the obligation.

There indeed results a most important difference, under our theory of government, as to the nature and character of the act itself, whether executed by the States themselves, or by their Governments; but a result, as I have already stated, not at all affecting the question under consideration, but which will throw much light on a subject, in relation to which I must think the Senator from Massachusetts has formed very confused conceptions. The Senator dwelt much on the point, that the present system is a Constitution and a Government, in contradistinction to the old confederation, with a view of proving that the constitution was not a compact. Now, I concede to the Senator, that our present system is a Constitution and a Government; and that the former, the old confederation, was not a Constitution or Government; not, however, for the reason which he assigned, that the former was a compact, and the latter not; but from the difference of the origin from which the two compacts are derived. According to our American conception, the people alone can form constitutions or Governments, and not their agents. It is this difference, and this alone, which makes the distinction. Had the old confederation been the act of the people of the several States, and not of their Governments, that instrument, imperfect as it was, would have been a constitution; and the agency which it created to execute its powers, a Government. This is the true cause of the difference between the two acts, and not that in which the Senator seems to be bewildered.

There is another point on which this difference throws important light, and which has been frequently referred to in debate on this and former occasions. I refer to the expression in the preamble of the Constitution, which speaks of "forming a more perfect union;" and in the letter of General Washington, laying the draught of the convention before the old Congress, in which he speaks of "consolidating the Union;" both of which I conceive to refer simply to the fact, that the present Union, as already stated, is a union between the States themselves, and not a union like that which had existed between the Governments of the States.

We will now proceed to consider some of the

conclusions which necessarily follow from the facts and positions already established. They enable us to decide a question of vital importance under our system: Where does sovereignty reside? If I have succeeded in establishing the fact that ours is a Federal system, as I conceive I conclusively have, that fact of itself determines the question which I have proposed. It is of the very essence of such a system, that the sovereignty is in the parts, and not in the whole; or, to use the language of Mr. Palgrave, "The parts are the units in such a system, and the whole the multiple; and not the whole the unit and the parts the fractions." Ours, then, is a Government of twenty-four Sovereignties, united by a constitutional compact, for the purpose of exercising certain powers through a common Government as their joint agent, and not a Union of the twenty-four Sovereignties into one, which, according to the language of the Virginia Resolutions, already cited, would form a Consolidation. And here I must express my surprise that the Senator from Virginia should avow himself the advocate of these very Resolutions, when he distinctly maintains the idea of a Union of the States in one Sovereignty, which is expressly condemned by these Resolutions as the essence of a consolidated Government.

Another consequence is equally clear, that, whatever modifications were made in the condition of the States under the present Constitution, they extended only to the exercise of their powers by compact, and not to the sovereignty itself, and are such as Sovereigns are competent to make: it being a conceded point, that it is competent to them to stipulate to exercise their powers in a particular manner, or to abstain altogether from their exercise, or to delegate them to agents, without in any degree impairing sovereignty itself. The plain state of the facts, as regards our Government, is, that these States have agreed by compact to exercise their sovereign powers jointly, as already stated; and that, for this purpose, they have ratified the compact in their sovereign capacity, thereby making it the constitution of each State, in nowise distinguished from their own separate constitutions, but in the super-added obligation of compact – of faith mutually pledged to each other. In this compact, they have stipulated, among other things, that it may be amended by three-fourths of the States: that is, they have conceded to each other by compact the right to add new powers or to subtract old, by the consent of that proportion of the States, without requiring, as otherwise would have been the case, the consent of all: a modification no more inconsistent, as has been supposed, with their sovereignty, than any other contained in the compact. In fact, the provision to which I allude furnishes strong evidence that the Sovereignty is, as I contend, in the States severally, as the amendments are effected, not by any one three-fourths, but by any three-fourths of the States, indicating that the sovereignty is in each of the States.

    If these views be correct, it follows, as a matter of course, that the allegiance of the people is to their several States, and that treason consists in resistance to the joint authority of the *States* united, not, as has been absurdly contended, in resistance to the Government of the United States, which, by the provision of the Constitution, has only the right of punishing.

Having now said what I intended in relation to my first Resolution, both in reply to the Senator from Massachusetts, and in vindication of its correctness, I will now proceed to consider the conclusions drawn from it in the second Resolution – that the General Government is not the exclusive and final judge of the extent of the powers delegated to it, but that the States, as parties to the compact, have a right to judge, in the last resort, of the infractions of the compact, and of the mode and measure of redress.

It can scarcely be necessary, before so enlightened a body, to premise that our system comprehends two distinct Governments – the General and State Governments, which, properly considered, form but one – the former representing the joint authority of the States in their confederate capacity, and the latter that of each State separately. I have premised this fact simply with a view of presenting distinctly the answer to the argument offered by the Senator from Massachusetts to prove that the General Government has a final and exclusive right to judge, not only of delegated powers, but also of those reserved to the States. That gentleman relies for his main argument on the assertion that a government, which he defines to be an organized body, endowed with both will, and power, and authority in *proprio vigore* to execute its purpose, has a right inherently to judge of its powers. It is not my intention to comment upon the definition of the Senator, though it would not be difficult to show that his ideas of Government are not very American. My object is to deal with the conclusion, and not the definition. Admit then, that the Government has the right of judging of its powers, for which he contends. Now, then, will he withhold, upon his own principle, the right of judging from the State Governments, which he has attributed to the General Government? If it belongs to one, on his principle, it belongs to both; and if to both, when they differ, the veto, so abhorred by the Senator, is the necessary result: as neither, if the right be possessed by both, can control the other.

The Senator felt the force of this argument, and, in order to sustain his main position, he fell back on that clause of the Constitution which provides that "this Constitution, and the laws made in pursuance thereof, shall be the supreme law of the land." This is admitted; no one has ever denied that the Constitution, and the laws made in *pursuance* of it, are of paramount authority. But it is equally undeniable that laws *not* made in pursuance are not only not of paramount authority, but are of no authority whatever, being of themselves null and void; which presents the question, who are to judge whether the laws be or be not pursuant to the Constitution? and thus the difficulty, instead of being taken away, is removed but one step further back. This the Senator also felt, and has attempted to overcome, by setting up, on the part of Congress and the Judiciary, the final and exclusive right of judging, both for the Federal Government and the States, as to the extent of their respective powers. That I may do full justice to the gentleman, I will give his doctrine in his own words. He states:

> That there is a supreme law, composed of the Constitution, the laws passed in pursuance of it, and the treaties; but in cases coming before Congress, not assuming the shape of cases in law and equity, so as to be subjects of judicial discussion, Congress must interpret the Constitution so often as it has occasion to pass laws; and in cases capable of assuming a judicial shape, the Supreme Court must be the final interpreter.

Now, passing over this vague and loose phraseology, I would ask the Senator upon what principle can he concede this extensive power to the Legislative and Judicial departments, and withhold it entirely from the Executive? If one has the right it cannot be withheld from the other. I would also ask him on what principle – if the departments of the General Government are to possess the right of judging, finally and conclusively, of their respective powers – on what principle can the same right be withheld from the State Governments, which, as well as the General Government, properly considered, are but departments of the same general system, and form together, properly speaking, but one Government? This was a favorite idea of Mr. Macon, for whose wisdom I have a respect increasing with my experience, and who I have frequently heard say, that most of the misconceptions and errors in relation to our system, originated in forgetting that they were but parts of the same system. I would further tell the Senator, that, if this right be withheld from the State Governments; if this restraining influence, by which the General Government is confined to its proper sphere, be withdrawn, then that department of the Government from which he has withheld the right of judging of its own powers (the Executive), will, so far from being excluded, become the *sole* interpreter of the powers of the Government. It is the *armed* interpreter, with powers to execute its own construction, and without the aid of which the construction of the other departments will be impotent.

But I contend that the States have a far clearer right to the sole construction of their powers than any of the departments of the Federal Government have. This power is expressly reserved, as I have stated on another occasion, not only against the several departments of the General Government, but against the United States themselves. I will not repeat the arguments which I then offered on this point, and which remain unanswered, but I must be permitted to offer strong additional proof of the views then taken, and which, if I am not mistaken, are conclusive on this point. It is drawn from the ratification of the Constitution by Virginia, and is in the following words:

> We, the Delegates of the people of Virginia, duly elected in pursuance of a recommendation from the General Assembly, and now met in Convention, having fully and freely investigated and discussed the proceedings of the Federal Convention, and being prepared, as well as the most mature deliberation hath enabled us, to decide thereon, do, in the name and in behalf of the people of Virginia, declare and make known that the powers granted under the Constitution, being derived from the people of the United States, may be resumed by them, whensoever the same shall be perverted to their injury or oppression, and that every power not granted thereby remains with them, and at their will; that, therefore, no right, of any denomination, can be cancelled, abridged, restrained, or modified, by the Congress, by the Senate or House of Representatives, acting in any capacity, by the President, or any department or officer of the United States, except in those instances in which power is given by the Constitution for those purposes; and that, among other essential rights, the liberty of conscience, and of the press, cannot be cancelled, abridged, restrained, or modified by any authority of the United States. With these impressions, with a solemn appeal to the Searcher of all hearts for the purity of our intentions, and under the conviction that whatsoever imperfections may exist in the Constitution ought rather to be examined in the mode prescribed therein, than to bring the Union in danger by a delay, with the hope of obtaining amendments previous to the ratifications, we, the said Dele-

gates, in the name and in the behalf of the people of Virginia, do, by these presents, assent to and ratify the Constitution recommended, on the 17th day of September, 1787, by the Federal Convention for the Government of the United States, hereby announcing to all those whom it may concern, that the said Constitution is binding upon the said people, according to an authentic copy hereto annexed, in the words following....

It thus appears that this sagacious State (I fear, however, that her sagacity is not so sharp-sighted now as formerly) ratified the Constitution, with an explanation as to her reserved powers; that they were powers subject to her own will, and reserved against every department of the General Government – Legislative, Executive, and Judicial – as if she had a prophetic knowledge of the attempts now made to impair and destroy them: which explanation can be considered in no other light than as containing a condition on which she ratified, and, in fact, making part of the Constitution of the United States – extending as well to the other States as herself. I am no lawyer, and it may appear to be presumption in me to lay down the rule of law which governs in such cases, in a controversy with so distinguished an advocate as the Senator from Massachusetts. But I shall venture to lay it down as a rule in such cases, which I have no fear that the gentleman will contradict, that, in case of a contract between several partners, if the entrance of one on condition be admitted, the condition enures to the benefit of all the partners.

But I do not rest the argument simply upon this view. Virginia proposed the tenth amended article, the one in question, and her ratification must be at least received as the highest evidence of its true meaning and interpretation.

If these views be correct – and I do not see how they can be resisted – the rights of the States to judge of the extent of their reserved powers stands on the most solid foundation, and is good against every department of the General Government; and the Judiciary is as much excluded from an interference with the reserved powers as the Legislative or Executive departments. To establish the opposite, the Senator relies upon the authority of Mr. Madison, in the *Federalist*, to prove that it was intended to invest the Court with the power in question. In reply, I will meet Mr. Madison with his own opinion, given on a most solemn occasion, and backed by the sagacious Commonwealth of Virginia. The opinion to which I allude will be found in the celebrated Report of 1799, of which Mr. Madison was the author. It says:

> But it is objected, that the judicial authority is to be regarded as *the sole expositor of the Constitution in the last resort*; and it may be asked for what reason the declaration by the General Assembly, supposing it to be theoretically true, could be required at the present day, and in so solemn a manner.
>
> On this objection it might be observed, *first*, that there may be instances of usurped power, which

the forms of the Constitution would never draw within the control of the Judicial department; *secondly*, that, if the decision of the judiciary be raised above the authority of the Sovereign parties to the Constitution, the decisions of the other departments, not carried by the forms of the Constitution before the judiciary, must be equally authoritative and final as the decisions of this department. But the proper answer to this objection is, that the Resolution of the General Assembly relates to those great and extraordinary cases in which all the forms of the Constitution may prove ineffectual against infractions dangerous to the essential rights of the parties to it. The Resolution supposes that dangerous powers, not delegated, may not only be usurped and executed by the other departments, but that the Judicial department, also, may exercise or sanction dangerous powers beyond the grant of the Constitution; and, consequently, that the ultimate right of the parties to the Constitution to judge whether the Compact was dangerously violated, must extend to violations by one delegated authority as well as by another; by the judiciary as well as by the executive or the Legislature.

But why should I waste words in reply to these or any other authorities, when it has been so clearly established that the rights of the States are reserved against each and every department of the Government, and no authority in opposition can possibly shake a position so well established? Nor do I think it necessary to repeat the argument which I offered when the bill was under discussion, to show that the clause in the Constitution which provides that the judicial power shall extend to all cases in law or equity arising under this Constitution, and to the laws and treaties made under its authority, has no bearing on the point in controversy; and that even the boasted power of the Supreme Court to decide a law to be unconstitutional, so far from being derived from this or any other portion of the Constitution, results from the necessity of the case – where two rules of unequal authority come in conflict – and is a power belonging to all courts, superior and inferior, State and General, Domestic, and Foreign.

I have now, I trust, shown satisfactorily, that there is no provision in the Constitution to authorize the General Government, through any of its departments, to control the action of a State within the sphere of its reserved powers; and that, of course, according to the principle laid down by the Senator from Massachusetts himself, the Government of the States, as well as the General Government, has the right to determine the extent of their respective powers, without the right on the part of either to control the other. The necessary result is the veto, to which he so much objects; and to get clear of which, he informed us, was the object for which the present Constitution was formed. I know not whence he has derived his information, but my impression is very different, as to the immediate motives which led to the formation of that instrument. I have always understood that the principle was, to give to Congress the power to regulate commerce, to lay impost duties, and to raise a revenue for the payment of the public debt and the expenses of the Government; and to subject the action of the citizens, individually, to the operation of the laws, as a substitute for force. If the object had been to get clear of the veto of the States, as the Senator states, the Convention, certainly, performed their work in a most bungling manner. There was, unquestionably, a large party in that body, headed by men of distinguished talents and influence, who commenced early and worked earnestly to the last, to deprive the States – not directly, for that would have been too bold an attempt, but indirectly – of the veto. The good sense of the Convention, however, put down every effort, however disguised and perseveringly made. I do not deem it necessary to give, from the journals, the history of these various and unsuccessful attempts – though it would afford a very instructive lesson. It is sufficient to say that it was attempted, by proposing to give to Congress power to annul the acts of the States which they might deem inconsistent with the Constitution; to give to the President the power of appointing the Governors of the States, with a view of vetoing State laws through his authority; and, finally, to give the Judiciary the power to decide controversies between the States and the General Government; all of which failed – fortunately for the liberty of the country – utterly and entirely failed; and in this failure we have the strongest evidence, that it was not the intention of the Convention to deprive the States of the veto power. Had the attempt to deprive them of this pow-

wer been directly made, and failed, every one would have seen and felt, that it would furnish conclusive evidence in favor of its existence. Now, I would ask, what possible difference can it make in what form this attempt was made? Whether by attempting to confer on the General Government a power incompatible with the exercise of the veto on the part of the States, or by attempting directly to deprive them of the right to exercise it? We have thus direct and strong proof that, in the opinion of the Convention, the States, unless deprived of it, possess the veto power – or, what is another name for the same thing, the right of nullification. I know that there is a diversity of opinion among the friends of State Rights in regard to this power, which I regret, as I cannot but consider it as a power essential to the protection of the minor and local interests of the community, and the liberty and the Union of the country. It is the very shield of State Rights, and the only power by which that system of injustice against which we have contended for more than thirteen years can be arrested: a system of hostile Legislation – of plundering by law, which must necessarily lead to a conflict of arms, if not prevented.

But I rest the right of a State to judge of the extent of its reserved powers, in the last resort, on higher grounds – that the Constitution is a compact, to which the States are parties in their Sovereign capacity; and that, as in all other cases of compact between parties having no common umpire, each has a right to judge for itself. To the truth of this proposition, the Senator from Massachusetts has himself assented, if the Constitution itself be a compact – and that it is, I have shown, I trust, beyond the possibility of a doubt. Having established this point, I now claim, as I stated I would do, in the course of the discussion, the admissions of the Senator, and, among them, the right of secession and nullification, which he conceded would necessarily follow if the Constitution be, indeed, a compact.

I have now replied to the arguments of the Senator from Massachusetts so far as they directly apply to the Resolutions, and will, in conclusion, notice some of his general and detached remarks. To prove that ours is a consolidated Government, and that there is an immediate connection between the Government and the citizen, he relies on the fact that the laws act directly on individuals. That such is the case I will not deny; but I am very far from conceding the point that it affords the decisive proof, or even any proof at all, of the position which the Senator wishes to maintain. I hold it to be perfectly within the competency of two or more States to subject their citizens, in certain cases, to the direct action of each other, without surrendering or impairing their sovereignty. I recollect, while I was a member of Mr. Monroe's cabinet, a proposition was submitted by the British Government to permit a mutual right of search and seizure, on the part of each Government, of the citizens of the other, on board of vessels engaged in the slave trade, and to establish a joint tribunal for their trial and punishment. The proposition was declined, not because it would impair the sovereignty of either, but on the ground of general expediency, and because it would be incompatible with the provisions of the Constitution which establish the judicial power, and which provisions require the judges to be appointed by the President and Senate. If I am not mistaken, propositions of the same kind were made and acceded to by some of the Continental powers.

With the same view the Senator cited the suability of the States as evidence of their want of sovereignty; at which I must express my surprise, coming from the quarter it does. No one knows better than the Senator that it is perfectly within the competency of a sovereign State to permit itself to be sued. We have on the statute-book a standing law, under which the United States may be sued in certain land cases. If the provision in the Constitution on this point proves any thing, it proves, by the extreme jealousy with which the right of suing a State is permitted, the very reverse of that for which the Senator contends.

Among other objections to the views of the Constitution for which I contend, it is said that they are novel. I hold this to be a great mistake. The novelty is not on my side, but on that of the Senator from Massachusetts. The doctrine of consolidation which he maintains is of recent growth. It is not the doctrine of Hamilton, Ames, or any of the distinguished Federalists of the period, all of whom strenuously maintained the Federative character of the

Constitution, though they were accused of supporting a system of policy which would necessarily lead to consolidation. The first disclosure of that doctrine was in the case of M'Culloch; in which the Supreme Court held the doctrine, though wrapped up in language somewhat indistinct and ambiguous. The next, and more open avowal, was by the Senator of Massachusetts himself, about three years ago, in the debate on Foote's resolution. The first official annunciation of the doctrine was in the recent proclamation of the President, of which the bill that has recently passed this body is the bitter fruit.

It is further objected by the Senator from Massachusetts, and others, against the doctrine of State Rights; as maintained in this debate, that, if it should prevail, the peace of the country would be destroyed. But what if it should not prevail? Would there be peace? Yes, the peace of despotism: that peace which is enforced by the bayonet and the sword; the peace of death, where all the vital functions of liberty have ceased. It is this peace which the doctrine of State Sovereignty may disturb by that conflict, which, in every free State, if properly organized, necessarily exists between liberty and power; but which, if restrained within proper limits, gives a salutary exercise to our moral and intellectual faculties. In the case of Carolina, which has caused all this discussion, who does not see if the effusion of blood be prevented, that the excitement, the agitation, and the inquiry which it has caused, will be followed by the most beneficial consequences? The country had sunk into avarice, intrigue, and electioneering – from which nothing but some such event could rouse it, or restore those honest and patriotic feelings which had almost disappeared under their baneful influence. What Government has ever attained power and distinction without such conflicts? Look at the degraded state of all those nations where they have been put down by the iron arm of the Government.

I, for my part, have no fear of any dangerous conflict, under the fullest acknowledgment of State Sovereignty: the very fact that the States may interpose will produce moderation and justice. The General Government will abstain from the exercise of any power in which they may suppose three-fourths of the States will not sustain them; while, on the other hand, the States will not interpose but on the conviction that they will be supported by one fourth of their co-States. Moderation and justice will produce confidence, attachment and patriotism; and these, in turn, will offer most powerful barriers against the excess of conflicts between the States and the General Government.

But we are told that, should the doctrine prevail, the present system would be as bad, if not worse, than the old Confederation. I regard the assertion only as evidence of that extravagance of declaration in which, from excitement of feeling, we so often indulge. Admit the power, and still the present system would be as far removed from the weakness of the old Confederation as it would be from the lawless and despotic violence of consolidation. So far from being the same, the difference between the Confederation and the present Constitution would still be most strongly marked. If there were no other distinction, the fact that the former required the concurrence of the States to execute its acts, and the latter, the act of a State to arrest them, would make a distinction as broad as the ocean. In the former, the *vis inertiae* of our nature is in opposition to the action of the system. Not to act was to defeat. In the latter the same principle is on the opposite side – action is required to defeat. He who understands human nature will see, in this fact alone, the difference between a feeble and illy-contrived Confederation, and the restrained energy of a Federal system. Of the same character is the objection that the doctrine will be the source of weakness. If we look to mere organization and physical power as the only source of strength, without taking into the estimate the operation of moral causes, such would appear to be the fact; but if we take into the estimate the latter, we shall find that those Governments have the greatest strength in which power has been most efficiently checked. The Government of Rome furnishes a memorable example. There, two independent and distinct powers existed – the people acting by Tribes, in which the Plebeians prevailed, and by Centuries, in which the Patricians ruled. The Tribunes were the appointed representatives of the one power, and the Senate of the other; each possessed of the authority of checking and overruling one another, not as departments of the Government, as supposed by the Senator from Massachusetts, but as independent powers – as much so as the State and General Governments. A shallow observer would perceive, in such an organization, nothing but the perpetual source of anarchy, discord, and weakness; and yet experience has proved that it was the most powerful Government that ever existed; and reason teaches that this power was derived from the very circumstances which hasty reflection would consider the cause of weakness. I will venture an assertion, which may be considered extravagant, but in which history will fully bear me out, that we have no knowledge of any people where the power of arresting the improper acts of the Government, or what may be called the negative power of Government, was too strong – except Poland, where every freeman possessed a veto. But even there, although it existed in so extravagant a form, it was the source of the highest and most lofty attachment to liberty, and the most heroic courage: qualities that more than once saved Europe from the domination of the crescent and cimeter. It is worthy of remark, that the fate of Poland is not to be attributed so much to the excess of this negative power of itself, as to the facility which it afforded to foreign influence in controlling its political movements.

I am not surprised that, with the idea of a perfect Government which the Senator from Massachusetts has formed – a Government of an absolute majority, unchecked and unrestrained, operating through a representative body – he should be so much shocked with what he is pleased to call the absurdity of the State *veto*. But let me tell him that his scheme of a perfect Government, as beautiful as he conceives it to be, though often tried, has invariably failed – has always run, whenever tried, through the same uniform process of faction, corruption, anarchy, and despotism. He considers the representative principle as the great modern improvement in legislation, and of itself sufficient to secure liberty. I cannot regard it in the light in which he does. Instead of modern, it is of remote origin, and has existed, in greater or less perfection, in every free State, from the remotest antiquity. Nor do I consider it as of itself sufficient to secure liberty, though I regard it as one of the indispensable means – the means of securing the people against the tyranny and oppression of their *rulers*. To secure liberty, another means is still necessary – the means of securing the different portions of society against the injustice and oppressions of each other, which can only be effected by *veto*, interposition, or nullification, or by whatever name the restraining or negative power of Government may be called.

APPENDIX THREE
The Constitutional Right of Secession
by James Spence

Secession is by no means a novel doctrine. In the first session of Congress under the new Constitution, it was threatened in the first serious contest that arose; and this in the presence of several of the framers of the Constitution. Again, when Washington expressed reluctance to be elected as President for a second term, Jefferson wrote to urge his assent; and the weightiest reason he assigned, in proof that the country required experience at the head of affairs, was this – that the coming election would involve great danger of a "secession from the Union" of those who should be defeated. It can hardly be supposed that this right would have been openly declared by members of Congress, or that the probability of the event would have been thus urged on Washington had it been regarded by public opinion as an illegal or treasonable act. It seems rather to be inferred that there existed in the minds of those, who with the facts so recent were most competent to

Thomas Jefferson

judge, a conviction that the right existed and might be exercised – that able and just government would avoid it – but still that it was there.

The doctrine, indeed, has been maintained and loudly declared, both in the North and South, at frequent periods in the history of the Union. Jefferson, in his *Ana*, refers to that occasion of its being first raised in Congress, and observes that it was the Eastern, that is, the Northern States, who especially threatened to secede. He describes a walk with Hamilton, in which the latter painted pathetically the danger of the secession of their members, and the separation of the States. And the Northern States were the first to raise it practically. The war of 1813 was highly unpopular in that district, and when called upon by the President to supply their quotas of militia, they absolutely declined. In the words of Jefferson to Lafayette: "During the war four of the Eastern States were only attached to the Union, like so many inanimate bodies to living men." But they went far beyond inaction. They called a Convention at Hartford, of which the proceedings were suppressed, but the object is well known; a flag appeared with five stripes, secession was threatened in the loudest terms, nor can there be a doubt in the mind of any one who studies the events of that period, that the New England States would have seceded from the Union had the war continued.

The State of Massachusetts has threatened, indeed, on four separate occasions to secede from the Union. First, in the debates referred to on the adjustment of the State debts; secondly, on the purchase of Louisiana and its admission into the Union; thirdly, during the war of 1813; and fourthly, on the annexation of Texas, when, we believe, one chamber of her legislature actually passed a vote of secession. On these occasions it was no mere act of excited individuals, but the general voice of the community. Yet this State is now the loudest in denouncing it, when inconvenient to herself; and a bastile is now said to be preparing in the vicinity of Boston, for the incarceration of those as political prisoners, who simply utter the opinions which, when it suited, this very State has so often and so vehemently expressed.

It has been a popular illustration with the advocates of the Union, that if a State may secede, so may a county from a State, or a town from a county, until society break up into chaos. The fallacy of this is very obvious. A State claims to secede in virtue of her right as a sovereignty. When a county becomes a sovereignty it may prefer an equal claim, but then it cannot be a county. The comparison fails in other respects. The secession of a State from others is the case of men who separate; the secession of a county would be that of a limb torn from the body. There is also no such practical danger as that which has been described. The secession of a single State would be suicidal; it would be surrounded with custom-houses, cramped with restrictions, and crushed under the expenses involved. North Carolina and Rhode Island, after refusing to join the Union, and holding out for more than two years, were at last constrained to accede, by the same causes which will always prevent any State from attempting to stand alone. Practically the right could not be exercised, even if conceded, except by a number of States together, sufficient in resources to enable them to maintain their position, and to endure the heavy cost of a separate government. Indeed, if justly governed, it is by no means clear why there should be any desire to secede.

A much more subtle argument was used by Jefferson, since often repeated. He observed that if one State claimed the right to secede from the rest, the others would have equal right to secede from one State, which would amount to turning it out of the Union. The argument is based on the assumption that a State, claiming the one, and objecting to the other, would exhibit a conflict of principles. But a State would protest against ejection because it involves compulsion; and she claims a right to retire, because if compelled to remain, that is equally a compulsory restraint. Both really involve the same principle; ejection and imprisonment are equally acts of compulsion: and this principle is alike objected to in both cases.

It has been argued that a State would thus claim the right to exercise her will against the others, whilst denying them the right to use their will as against herself. But the case is not one of will within the limit of individual action, but of compulsion extending to, and exercised over, another. A State compelled to go or to remain has a forcible restraint imposed on its will; but in seceding it imposes no restraint on the will of others – they remain free to follow, or continue as before.

It has been urged that reasonable men would not have formed a system exposed to ruin at any time by the secession of its constituents. But the question is not whether the terms of the compact were wise or prudent, but simply what those terms are, and the force they possess. Men make injudicious wills, but these cannot be disputed on the ground of their narrow wisdom. The argument ignores, too, the facts which surrounded the framing of the Constitution. It was the result of a series of compromises. Hence that which may appear unreasonable for any community to have enacted for itself, is reasonable enough when viewed correctly, as the best system it was possible to compass under the circumstances.

Much stress has been laid on the term "supreme," as applied to the Federal laws. In reality their only supremacy is in extent – in extending throughout the whole country, whilst the action of a State law is confined within its boundaries. Apart from this, the State is as supreme as the Federal law. No question exists of relative rank, of any superiority; each is supreme in its own department, both are equally powerless beyond it. The Federal Government has indeed no absolute law-making power; for all its laws are liable to be declared void by the Supreme Court. That Court declared null and void the most important law ever passed by the Federal legislature – the Missouri compromise. It sits not merely as the interpreter, but as the judge of the law.

It has been argued that the present Constitution differs in principle from the Articles of Confederation, in enabling the Federal Government to act directly on individuals, instead of doing so through the State governments. The inference is drawn that the sovereignty of the States has been surrendered by this concession. Had such a right been committed to a foreign Government, or to any substantive power, this might have been a natural inference. But the Federal Government has no substantive power, and is only the joint agent of the States. These act directly on their own citizens, each through its special government or agent, in the great majority of cases. They agree to act on them through the Federal or common agent in certain other specified cases. This is simply a more effective manner of procedure, a question of detail, greatly improving the administration, but affecting in nowise the question of sovereignty. Further, it was pointed out by Madison in the Convention that the principle itself was not new, but existed under the Articles of Confederation, in several cases which he specified.

A federal republic is a partnership of republics. It has been argued that, admitting this to be the case, still, when once formed, it could not be dissolved by one without the consent of the others. But a very common form of partnership, in this and other countries, is partnership at will; from this any one party may retire without consulting the rest. And it seems to have escaped observation, how much wider are the powers of a sovereign State than those of a private individual. To a partnership of States the words of Madison apply: "When resort can be had to no common superior, the parties to the compact must themselves be the rightful judges, whether the bargain has been pursued or violated."

It has, indeed, been contended that the principles of a partnership at will could not apply, because this was to last for ever. On the point of duration the Constitution is silent, except in what is merely the expression of a desire, in the preamble, "to secure the blessings of liberty to ourselves and our posterity." On this subject there is no enactment or injunction. But on turning to the previous Articles of Confederation, we find in the title the words "perpetual union," and in the body, the express injunction – "And the union shall be perpetual." On this point they clearly possessed greater force than that of the Constitution; yet, notwithstanding this, they were terminated at the end of a few years, and that, too, with liberty to any State to leave the Federation altogether. The Union has, therefore, proved, by its own act, that terms of this nature have no force of law, but simply indicate the intention and the desire of the parties at the time. We find, too, that the Federal Government entered into a close alliance with France, the terms of which strongly enjoined that it should last for ever; yet these terms were held to be no obstacle to annulling it, without the consent of the other party.

On turning to the Constitution, it causes surprise to find that no prohibition of secession exists in it. Those who framed it were men well versed in public affairs, surrounded by angry passions, employed in the very act of breaking up a Constitution, if, indeed, it may not be said, of seceding from one of the States, for Rhode Island continued to adhere to it. They provided for a State dividing into two or more – for several uniting into one – for the admission of States yet to come into existence. Why, then, this remarkable omission? A contingency far more probable than these was that of a State becoming dissatisfied, and desiring to separate. Was such an omission the result of negligence, of inability to foresee so probable an event, or was it the result of design?

It has been contended that it would have been improper to forbid a State to withdraw – that it would have been "futile and undignified" to have added to a law, "And be it further enacted that the said law shall not be violated." But this is just what all law has to do; and that which does it not, is not law. Who had the powers of a lawgiver over independent, sovereign States, entering into a compact of their own free will? And where is the law, either to be violated or obeyed? There is a provision for a State separating into pieces, and this appears quite as undignified as to provide against a State, whole and intact, separating from the rest. There is provision against the treason of individuals; and if a State can also commit treason, it would be strange law that provided against crime on a small scale, omitting to deal with it when on a large one. The men who framed the Constitution were eminently practical men. It cannot be supposed that they would slight so formidable a danger. Why, then, the omission? For the soundest and wisest reasons, which we have on record from their own lips.

In the first place, had there been inserted in the Constitution a compulsory clause of this nature, it would have been impossible to obtain the ratification of the States. Very difficult, at the present day, would it be to obtain the assent to such a clause even of the Northern States. Theoretically nothing would be easier, but when it came to the point, it would hardly be possible to prevail upon Massachusetts, even at this day, to abandon, for ever, her often-asserted independence and sovereignty, and accept, in reality and truth, that position in which she is said now to exist – that of the province of a wider power. And if there would now be such practical difficulty, with the State whose present professions are those most favourable to the step, how great would have been the obstacles when all the States were to be included, many hostile to, and jealous of, the rest, and when the task was regarded, and proved to be, all but impossible, without this further and strong element of repugnance?

In the next place, the framers of the Constitution perceived, that should they forbid the retirement of a State, they must provide means to prevent it; otherwise it would be an idle precept, a mere solicitation to remain. Other questions might be referred to the Supreme Court, but a retiring State withdrew from its jurisdiction. Other forms of delinquency could be visited on individuals, but here was the action of a whole community. Goodwill must have died out before it could occur; argument would be vain; there could be no appeal except to force. But no force was to be created, adequate to an undertaking of this nature. The first act under the Constitution for regulating the military establishment, provided for a standing force of only 1,216 rank and file. True, in case of need this might be increased; but a cardinal principle with the people was to distrust standing armies; a subject on which their feeling was jealous in the extreme. It was impracticable to run counter to this, even so far as to provide the framework of an army equal to such an object. The only possible force would be that of the remaining States, to be employed in coercing those that desired to secede. On such a proposition the views of the two chief framers of the Constitution are on record. In the Convention, on the 31st May, 1787, Madison declared that "the use of force against a State would be more like a declaration of war, than an infliction of punishment, and would probably be considered by the party attacked, as a dissolution of all previous compacts; a union of States containing such an ingredient seemed to provide for its own destruction." Again, on the 8th June, he observed: "Any government formed on the supposed practicability of using force against the unconstitutional proceedings of the

States, would prove as visionary and fallacious as the government of Congress."

Hamilton, in that great authority the *Federalist*, after showing the futility of employing force against a State, concludes thus:

> When the sword is once drawn the passions of men observe no bounds of moderation. The suggestions of wounded pride, the instigations of resentment, would be apt to carry the States against which the arms of the Union were exerted, to any extreme to avenge the affront, or to avoid the disgrace of submission. The first war of this kind would probably terminate in a dissolution of the Union.

In one of the debates in the New York State Convention, Hamilton made use of these words: "To coerce a State would be one of the maddest projects ever devised. No State would ever suffer itself to be used as the instrument of coercing another." His far-seeing description in the *Federalist* is but too applicable to the events of the present day; and remarkable it is that he, the master spirit of the Unionists, should have denounced as "madness" that coercion which is adopted by his followers at the present day.

But there was a consideration of still higher import. The Constitution was a voluntary act, framed on the principles of free, mutual assent, and common belief in its advantages. To introduce force as a means of maintaining it, would be repugnant to these principles. It would be a commencement on the voluntary system, to be continued under compulsion.

Force is an attribute of monarchy; the throne represents and wields the strength of the nation. Each part is subservient to the whole, and none can revolt without foreknowledge of this force to encounter and overthrow. But the basis of a Federal Republic is the reverse of all this. It stands upon consent, which is the abnegation of force. In place of submission of part to the whole, the parties are co-equal. Compulsion is not only inapplicable, but opposed to the principle of the system. And the men of that day were too logical to be unaware of this; they declined to incorporate with the structure they were rearing a principle directly antagonistic to it.

There is another great constitutional authority, the fountain head of American politics – the Declaration of Independence – of which the first clause bears directly on this question:

> We hold these truths to be self-evident: that all men are created equal; that they are endowed by their Creator with certain inalienable rights; that amongst these are life, liberty, and the pursuit of happiness; that to secure these rights, governments are instituted among men, deriving their just powers from the consent of the governed; that whenever any form of government becomes destructive to these ends, it is the right of the people to alter, or abolish it.

These are the constitutional principles for the guidance of every citizen. When the people of Georgia, left in doubt by the silence of the Federal compact on the subject of secession, refer to these to enlighten them, to what conclusion must they come – what hesitation can they feel? They are told that the "pursuit of happiness" is "an inalienable right of man"; they feel that the government over them has become "destructive of this end"; they read that thereupon "it is the right of the people to alter or abolish it." It will, indeed, be said that the people referred to, are the whole people of the whole country, but this is not the fact. That, indeed, may promote the happiness of Georgia, which produces woe in California, at a distance of three thousand five hundred miles. By what arithmetic can the balance of happiness be adjusted between them? Further, the Declaration of Independence did not speak for all the people under the rule it denounced, but for a small portion of them only; nor did it speak for the people of the United States as a single people, but as separate colonies now claiming to be independent, the respective, original States. Clearly, then, this language is adopted by the people of each separate colony now a State, having a form of government over it of which it is to judge, and which, whenever so disposed, it may abolish.

Again, governments are unjust unless their powers are based on the "consent of the governed." Here the same question arises, Who are the governed who are to consent? Are the people of the State of Georgia to refrain from dissenting until they agree with the people of Oregon, more remote than England from Arabia? But this principle also was enunciated, like the last, for the guidance of each separate, distinct community. Upon these principles we can arrive at no other conclusions than these – that according to the constitutional doctrines of America, whenever a State decides by the vote of a majority of its people, that the government over it has become destructive to the ends of its welfare and happiness, and no longer exists in its consent, such State has a right to abolish that government, so far as it concerns itself, or, in other words, has a right to secede from the Union.

BIBLIOGRAPHY

☆ ☆ ☆ ☆

Benton, Thomas Hart (editor), *Abridgment of the Debates of Congress 1789 to 1856* (New York: D. Appleton and Company, 1857).

Bledsoe, Albert Taylor, *Is Davis a Traitor?* (Richmond, Virginia: The Hermitage Press, Inc., 1907).

Carey, Matthew (editor), *The American Museum: Repository of Ancient and Modern Fugitive Pieces* (Philadelphia, Pennsylvania: Self-published, 1788).

Carey, Matthew, *The Olive Branch* (Philadelphia, Pennsylvania: M. Carey and Son, 1818).

Carpenter, Stephen D., *The Logic of History: Five Hundred Political Texts Being Concentrated Extracts of Abolitionism* (Madison, Wisconson: Self-published, 1864).

Cooley, Thomas M., *Michigan: A History of Governments* (Boston: Houghton, Mifflin and Company, 1895).

Curtis, George Ticknor, *History of the Origin, Formation, and Adoption of the Constitution of the United States* (New York: Harper and Brothers, 1855).

Curtis, George Ticknor, *Life of James Buchanan, Fifteenth President of the United States* (New York: D. Appleton and Company, 1883).

Davis, Jefferson, *The Rise and Fall of the Confederate Government* (New York: D. Appleton and Company, 1881).

Dickinson, John, *The Political Writings of John Dickinson, Esquire* (Wilmington, Delaware: Bonsol and Niles, 1801).

Edmonds, George (Elizabeth Meriwether), *Facts and Falsehoods Concerning the War on the South 1861-65* (Memphis, Tennessee: A.R. Taylor and Company, 1904).

Elliott, Jonathan (editor), *Journal and Debates of the Federal Convention* (Washington, D.C.: self-published, 1836).

Elliott, Jonathan (editor), *The Debates in the Several State Conventions on the Adoption of the Federal Constitution* (Washington, D.C.: self-published, 1837).

Max Farrand (editor), *The Records of the Federal Convention of 1787* (New Haven, Connecticut: Yale University Press, 1911).

Fehrenbach, T.R., *Greatness to Spare* (Princeton, New Jersey: D. Van Nostrand, 1968).

Fowl, William Bentley, *The Free Speaker: A New Collection of Pieces For Declamation Original as Well as Selected* (Boston: Self-Published, 1859).

Freeman, Douglas Southall, *R. E. Lee: A Biography* (New York: Charles Scribner's Sons, 1935).

Greeley, Horace, *American Conflict* (Hartford, Connecticut: O.D. Chase, 1866).

Helper, Hinton Rowan, *The Impending Crisis: How to Meet It* (New York: A.B. Burdick, Publishers, 1857).

Landon, Judson A., *The Constitutional History and Government of the United States* (Boston: Houghton, Mifflin and Company, 1905).

Lieber, Francis, *Civil Liberty and Self Government* (Philadelphia, Pennsylvania: J.B. Lippincott and Company, 1859).

Lodge, Henry Cabot, *Daniel Webster* (Boston: Houghton, Mifflin, and Company, 1899).

Lunt, George, *The Origin of the Late War* (New York: D. Appleton and Company, 1866).

McGuire, Hunter and Christian, George L., *The Confederate Cause and Conduct in the War Between the States* (Richmond, Virginia: L. H. Jenkins, Inc., 1907).

McHenry, George, *The Cotton Trade: Its Bearing Upon the Prosperity of Great Britain and Commerce of the American Republics* (London: Saunders, Otley, and Company, 1863).

McKee, Thomas Hudson, *National Conventions and Platforms of All Political Parties 1789-1900* (Baltimore, Maryland: Friedenwald Company, 1900).

McPherson, James M., *Abraham Lincoln and the Second American Revolution* (New York: Oxford University Press, 1990).

Meyers, Marvin (editor), *The Mind of the Founder: Sources of the Political Thought of James Madison* (Indianapolis, Indiana: The Bobbs-Merrill Company, 1973).

Nicolay, John G. and Hay, John, *Abraham Lincoln: Complete Works* (New York: The Century Company, 1984).

Phillips, Wendell, *Speeches, Lectures, and Letters* (Boston: Walker, Wise and Company, 1864).

Pitkin, Timothy, *A Political and Civil History of the United States From the Year 1763 to the Close of the Administration of Washington in March 1797* (New Haven, Connecticut: Hezekiah Howe, and Durrie and Peck, 1828).

Rawle, William, *A View of the Constitution of United*

States of America (Philadelphia, Pennsylvania: Philip H. Nicklin and Company, 1829).

Richardson, James D. (editor), *A Compilation of the Messages and Papers of the Presidents* (Washington, D. C.: Bureau of National Literature, 1922).

Sage, Bernard Janin, *The Republic of Republics: A Retrospect of Our Century of Federal Liberty* (Philadelphia, Pennsylvania: William W. Harding, 1878).

Scott, John, *The Lost Principle: The Sectional Equilibrium, How It Was Created, How It Was Destroyed, and How It May Be Restored* (Richmond, Virginia: James Woodhouse and Company, 1860).

Sparks, Jared, *Life of Gouverneur Morris With Selections From His Correspondence and Miscellaneous Papers* (Boston: Gary and Bowen, 1832).

Spence, James, *The American Union: Its Effect on National Character and Policy* (London: Richard Bentley and Son, 1862).

Stark, James Henry, *The Loyalists of Massachusetts and the Other Side of the American Revolution* (Boston: Self-Published, 1910).

Story, Joseph, *Commentaries on the Constitution* (Boston: Hilliard, Gray and Company, 1833).

Upshur, Abel Parker, *The True Nature and Character of Our Federal Government* (New York: Van Evrie, Horton and Company, [1840] 1868).

Vattel, Emmerich de, *The Law of Nations: Principles of the Law of Nature Applied to the Conduct and Affairs of Nations and Sovereigns* (New York: Samuel Campbell, 1796).

Daniel Webster, *A Memorial to the Congress of the Unit-*

ed States on the Subject of Restraining the Increase of Slavery in New States to be Admitted Into the Union (Boston: Sewell Phelps, 1819).

Made in the USA
Columbia, SC
06 October 2022

68515812R00089